Regulating Micro-aggressions

Comparative Discrimination Law

The titles published in this series are listed at *brill.com/rpcds*

Regulating Micro-aggressions

The Legal Challenge of Everyday Bias

By

Anton Kok
Lee-Anne Germanos Manuel

BRILL | NIJHOFF

ISSN 2452-2023
ISBN 978-90-04-75751-6
ISBN 978-90-04-75752-3 (PDF)
DOI https://doi.org/10.1163/9789004757523

Library of Congress Control Number: 2026943545

Brill Nijhoff and Koninklijke Brill BV are part of De Gruyter Brill.
www.degruyterbrill.com

Questions about General Product Safety Regulation: productsafety@degruyterbrill.com

Contents

CHAPTER 1

Introduction

> It was not usually the big things, the awful atrocities, that got at you. No, it was the daily pinpricks, the little discourtesies, the minute humiliations, having one's dignity trodden underfoot, not always with jackboots – though that happened too. It was, for instance, on occasions like going into a shop with your father, this dignified, educated man who headed up a school, and a slip of a girl behind the counter, just because she was white, would address your father, 'Ja, boy.' ... This kind of treatment gnawed away at your very vitals.[1]

> While writing this post, I really thought about whether or not I should detail some of my experiences with racism in parts of Europe but I thought for my own sanity and emotional well being rather I not. I also have every intention to continue enjoying my experience here but wow it can be hard. But I will say this, nothing in the books about theories of racism, theories of difference and otherness, violence etc. prepared me for how it would feel to have to stomach it, for how it would feel to say nothing where naturally you would otherwise be able to stand up for yourself. I knew I would be confronted with it and I knew I would have to keep quiet but I never thought about what it would feel like. You're not at home and you can't choose the spaces you can be in. There's nowhere for you to "escape", to be around people that look like you, or who won't constantly scrutinize you, make you an object unprovoked. Moments after I swallow it I think about whether what I think happened is indeed the case, there's no referent to go to say "hey bra has this ever happened to you? I'm not crazy right?" Especially because the racism isn't grand and blatant. It's in interpersonal discussions, it's momentary, it's masked with curiosity and endearment. It hurts. It doesn't happen all the time here and not all the people here are this way (this isn't a qualifier of sorts it's simply the case) but this doesn't make it any less painful. I have my family and friends to talk to about it so that helps but tjesses abelengu joh.[2]

In this book, we explore the phenomenon of micro-aggressions – subtle, often normalised, and seemingly trivial acts of discrimination that cumulatively undermine dignity and equality. We ask whether legal systems should recognise and respond to these "daily pinpricks," or whether they ought to be dismissed under the maxim *de minimis non curat lex*. Our analysis of micro-aggressions

1 Tutu (1999) 74 (Archbishop Desmond Tutu, reflecting on the apartheid era).
2 Facebook post of a Facebook friend, posted 4 May 2019.

 | HTTPS://DOI.ORG/10.1163/9789004757523-002

is primarily situated within the South African constitutional and legislative framework, particularly the Promotion of Equality and Prevention of Unfair Discrimination Act.[3] South Africa's past is marked not only by systemic state oppression, marginalisation, and violence, but also by the daily, "small" humiliations endured by the majority black population. It is therefore valuable to consider how the post-1994 South African Parliament and courts have responded to this legacy. What role has state law, through legislation and judicial decisions, played in addressing these everyday indignities, and where might it have fallen short? A comparative survey of the treatment of micro-aggressions in Germany, Canada, New Zealand, the Netherlands, and Namibia highlights that there is little appetite in national legislatures and courts to address subtle discrimination. The South African legal system's response to micro-aggressions has been somewhat incoherent, as will appear from our analysis below.

Micro-aggressions highlight the intersection between law, psychology, and social practice in understanding and responding to forms of harm that are frequently dismissed as trivial or unintentional. We argue that legal systems (legislatures and courts) should not too easily dismiss micro-aggressions as too trivial to warrant attention. We situate our discussion within the vision of a constitutionally-mandated kind and caring society (at least in the case of South Africa). We examine the role of law in shaping social interactions and consider whether dismissing small acts of exclusion risks entrenching patterns of marginalisation and inequality.

We offer a brief conceptualisation of micro-aggressions, drawing mainly from psychology. The analysis proceeds to an analysis of selected legal frameworks. Building on these insights, the book advances proposals for reform. It argues for a multi-layered response: embedding equality education in schools, requiring institutions to develop equality plans, and ensuring that courts and human rights bodies recognise the cumulative harms of subtle exclusion. Addressing micro-aggressions is not merely about protecting individuals from harm (after the fact, in courts) but about advancing substantive equality, dismantling systemic patterns of exclusion, and cultivating environments in which diversity is genuinely celebrated.

The book proceeds as follows. Chapter 2 provides a brief conceptualisation of micro-aggressions. Chapter 3 makes the case for the legal recognition of micro-aggressions. In chapter 4, we offer a snapshot of how *de minimis not curat lex* tends to play out in courts. We consider (i) general principles that tend to apply; (ii) the relevance of this maxim in constitutional litigation; and (iii) the outcome of litigation in South African lower courts and High Courts,

3 Act 4 of 2000 ("the South African Equality Act").

where *de minimis* may have come into play. Chapter 5 provides a brief overview of national anti-discrimination legislation in the indicated countries. We consider the extent to which these national laws allow for a *de minimis* defence. In chapter 6, we consider the South African Equality Act in more detail. We point out that this Act is explicitly a transformational piece of legislation that has the creation of a kind and caring South African society as one of its aims. We describe the causes of action recognised in this Act (hate speech, harassment and unfair discrimination). We consider the interplay between the various internal limitations in these causes of action with *de minimis*, with a particular focus on hate speech. As we show below, the South African Constitutional Court blows hot and cold in addressing micro-aggressions. In light of the outcome of the comparative survey (that legislatures and courts are too ambivalent in relation to micro-aggressions), we offer a few ways forward in the final chapter.

CHAPTER 2

Conceptualising Micro-aggressions

Micro-aggressions may variously be described as "every day verbal, nonverbal and environmental slights, snubs, or insults, whether intentional or unintentional, which communicate hostile, derogatory, or negative messages to target persons based solely upon their marginalized group membership";[1] or words or conduct that "may on the surface appear quite harmless, trivial, a small slight, but have a powerful impact on psychological well-being of marginalised groups";[2] or "brief, everyday exchanges that send denigrating messages to people of colour because they belong to a racial minority group".[3]

The term "micro-aggression" seems to have been first used in 1978 by Pierce to describe "subtle, stunning, often automatic, and non-verbal exchanges which are 'put downs'".[4] Sue has, along with colleagues, defined and exemplified this occurrence, primarily relating to psychology and the clinical practice thereof.[5] A micro-aggression does not have to be perpetrated intentionally or consciously, and the "offender" does not have to be purposefully hostile.[6]

Table 1 below construed by Sue *et al* depicts the nine themes found in micro-aggressions.[7] These themes are clearly not a closed list, and some micro-aggressions will probably fall outside these themes.

TABLE 1 The nine themes of micro-aggressions based on Sue *et al* (2007)

Theme	Micro-aggression	Message
Alien in own land When Asian Americans and Latino Americans are assumed to be foreign-born	"Where are you from?" "Where were you born?" "You speak good English." A person asking an Asian American to teach them words in their native language.	You are not American. You are a foreigner

1 Sue (2010) *Psychology Today.*
2 Ibid.
3 Sue *et al* (2007) 62 *American Psychologist* 271 272.
4 Pierce (1978) 62–68.
5 Sue *et al* (2007) 62 *American Psychologist* 271.
6 Ibid 274.
7 Ibid 272–276.

 | HTTPS://DOI.ORG/10.1163/9789004757523-003

TABLE 1 The nine themes of micro-aggressions based on Sue *et al* (2007) (*cont.*)

Theme	Micro-aggression	Message
Ascription of Intelligence Assigning intelligence to a person of colour on the basis of their race.	"You are a credit to your race." "You are so articulate." Asking an Asian person to help with a Math or Science problem.	People of colour are generally not as intelligent as whites. It is unusual for someone of your race to be intelligent. All Asians are intelligent and good in Math / Sciences.
Colour Blindness Statements that indicate that a White person does not want to acknowledge race	"When I look at you, I don't see colour." "America is a melting pot." "There is only one race, the human race."	Denying a person of colour's racial / ethnic experiences. Assimilate / acculturate to the dominant culture. Denying the individual as a racial / cultural being.
Criminality – assumption of criminal status A person of colour is presumed to be dangerous, criminal, or deviant on the basis of their race.	A white man or woman clutching their purse or checking their wallet as a Black or Latino approaches or passes. A store owner following a customer of colour around the store. A white person waits to ride the next elevator when a person of colour is on it.	You are a criminal. You are going to steal / You are poor / You do not belong / You are dangerous.
Denial of individual racism A statement made when whites deny their racial biases	"I'm not a racist. I have several Black friends." "As a woman, I know what you go through as a racial minority."	I am immune to races because I have friends of colour. Your racial oppression is no different than my gender oppression. I can't be a racist. I'm like you.

TABLE 1 The nine themes of micro-aggressions based on Sue *et al* (2007) (*cont.*)

Theme	Micro-aggression	Message
Myth of meritocracy Statements which assert that race does not play a role in life successes	"I believe the most qualified person should get the job." "Everyone can succeed in this society, if they work hard enough."	People of colour are given extra unfair benefits because of their race. People of colour are lazy and / or incompetent and need to work harder.
Pathologizing cultural values / communication styles The notion that the values and communication styles of the dominant / white culture are ideal	Asking a Black person: "Why do you have to be so loud / animated? Just calm down." To an Asian or Latino person: Why are you so quiet? We want to know what you think. Be more verbal." Speak up more." Dismissing an individual who brings up race / culture in work / school setting.	Assimilate to dominant culture. Leave your cultural baggage outside.
Second-class citizen Occurs when a white person is given preferential treatment as a consumer over a person of colour	Person of colour mistaken for a service worker Having a taxi cab pass a person of colour and pick up a white passenger being ignored at a store counter as attention is given to the white customer behind you "You people ..."	People of colour are servants to whites. They couldn't possibly occupy high-status positions. You are likely to cause trouble and / or travel to a dangerous neighbourhood. Whites are more valued customers than people of colour You don't belong. You are a lesser being.

TABLE 1 The nine themes of micro-aggressions based on Sue *et al* (2007) (*cont.*)

Theme	Micro-aggression	Message
Environmental micro-aggressions Macro-level micro-aggressions, which are more apparent on systemic and environmental levels	A college or university with buildings that are all names after white heterosexual upper class males Television shows and movies that feature predominantly white people, without representation of people of colour Overcrowding of public schools in communities of colour Overabundance of liquor stores in communities of colour	You don't belong / You won't succeed here. There is only so far you can go. You are an outsider / You don't exist. People of colour don't / shouldn't value education. People of colour are deviant.
How to offend without really trying	"Indian giver." "That's so gay." "She welshed on the bet." "I jewed him down." "That's so White of you." "You people ..." "We got gypped." Imitating accents or dialects	

CHAPTER 3

Making the Case for the Legal Recognition of Micro-aggressions

We take it as self-evident that a kind and caring society is preferable to a nasty and brutish one. If we have to offer some common-sense justification for this view, several reasons can easily be given. A kind society respects and upholds the dignity and rights of individuals. This is aligned with the principles of many ethical frameworks, including human rights, which emphasise the inherent worth of every person. Kindness and caring are rooted in empathy and compassion, fostering a sense of connection and mutual respect among individuals. A supportive and caring society promotes better mental health and well-being. People feel safer and more valued, consequently reducing stress, anxiety, and depression. Kindness and care strengthen social bonds and community ties. People are more likely to cooperate and support each other, leading to a more harmonious and cohesive society. A caring society discourages violence and conflict, leading to a more peaceful environment where individuals can thrive without fear. A supportive environment encourages productivity and innovation. People are more willing to take risks and be creative when they feel supported and valued. A caring society invests in public health and social services, leading to better overall health outcomes and reduced healthcare costs. Societies that care for their members tend to have more stable economies. Reduced crime, better health, and stronger social cohesion contribute to a more resilient and robust economy. A society built on kindness and care is more resilient in the face of crises. People are more likely to come together and support one another during difficult times. Caring societies are more likely to prioritise sustainable development, ensuring that resources are managed responsibly for future generations.

In contrast, a nasty and brutish society is characterised by conflict, distrust, and a lack of empathy. This leads to numerous negative outcomes. A lack of care and respect for others fosters violence and crime, making society less safe and more chaotic. High levels of stress, fear, and anxiety prevail in such societies, leading to widespread mental health problems. Distrust and hostility erode social bonds, leading to isolation and fragmentation within the community. The instability and conflict in a brutish society hinder economic growth and development, resulting in poverty and inequality. Lack of investment in public health and social services leads to poor health outcomes and increased

 | HTTPS://DOI.ORG/10.1163/9789004757523-004

healthcare costs. Ultimately, a kind and caring society not only aligns with ethical principles but also creates a more stable, prosperous, and sustainable environment for everyone.[1]

In this book, we deal with a small subset of what it means to live in a kind and caring society: how we relate to one another, how we speak to one another and how we conduct ourselves in others' company. More specifically, we ask if legal systems have a role to play in facilitating the creation of a kind and caring society. If an unkind word is spoken or someone behaves rudely, when should legal recourse be possible?

We consider whether there is such a thing as trivial, insulting speech or hate speech, or trivial harassment, or trivial discrimination. It may happen that the complainant will shrug off the particular incident as too small to take any formal steps to address the incident, but should a particular complainant bring the matter to a court's attention, should it be open to a court to brand incidents of this nature as too trivial to adjudicate? And if a court should not adjudicate these "daily pinpricks", should a legal system in some other way address these infractions?

Many jurisdictions recognise the maxim *de minimis non curat lex*, or some variant of this principle – that the law does not concern itself with, or does not have regard to, trivialities. Should this maxim apply to cases of discrimination, hate speech and harassment? In *R v Walton*,[2] the court suggested that "in the ordinary hurly-burly of everyday life a man (sic) must be expected to endure minor or trivial insults to his dignity". If this is true, should the same apply to discrimination, hate speech and harassment? Dismissing such conduct as legally irrelevant under the *de minimis* principle risks overlooking the ways in which micro-aggressions erode dignity, normalise marginalisation, and perpetuate inequality.

We address discrimination, hate speech and harassment in this book as these terms are probably the closest approximations as to how a lawyer would describe micro-aggressions. For example, these three causes of action are recognised in the South African Equality Act. The South African Parliament promulgated the Equality Act pursuant to section 9(4) of the Constitution.[3] This

1 If it is necessary to provide some sources for this view, see Archer (2024) Psychreg https://www.psychreg.org/10-benefits-kindness/ (accessed 5 September 2024), Schiller (2023) UNC Health Talk https://healthtalk.unchealthcare.org/kindness-can-be-positively-powerful-heres-why/ (accessed 5 September 2025), and Hanley-Dafoe (2023) https://www.psychologytoday.com/us/blog/everyday-resilience/202303/the-remarkable-power-of-kindness-and-why-it-matters (accessed 5 September 2025).

2 1958 3 SA 693 (SR) 695.

3 Constitution of the Republic of South Africa, 1996 (hereafter "South African Constitution").

section states that "no person may unfairly discriminate directly or indirectly against anyone on one or more grounds in terms of subsection (3). *National legislation must be enacted to prevent or prohibit unfair discrimination*" (emphasis added). On a narrow reading of section 9(4), this national law had to flesh out the prohibition of unfair discrimination on the horizontal plane. The legislature went further. It also outlawed hate speech and harassment, and drafted a chapter in the Equality Act that deals with the promotion of equality. This South African version of anti-discrimination legislation therefore treats harassment and hate speech as self-standing causes of action, not as subsets of (unfair) discrimination. Each of these causes of action has its own self-standing definition and defences. The same incident could therefore amount to (unfair) discrimination, hate speech and harassment – although questions could then be asked about a duplication of the causes of action.[4]

We set out an argument in this book that the maxim *de minimis non curat lex* should not apply to these causes of action, or at the very least that legal systems should recognise these causes of action in some way, and provide for some legal remedy (for example, in the form of the obligatory preparation and publishing of equality plans). In the legal definitions of discrimination, hate speech and harassment, there are usually internal qualifiers that already raise the risk that *de minimis* may implicitly be in play, without necessarily explicitly invoking the maxim – "unfair" for discrimination, "persistent" or "serious" for harassment, "hurtful" or "harmful" for hate speech, and so on. We argue why courts should be astute not to rely on "triviality" to non-suit a plaintiff. In the alternative, a different route is suggested in the last section of this book on how a legal system could also address micro-aggressions (in other words, outside of litigation).

There are obviously opposing views. When the university where one of the authors teaches operationalised its new policy on discrimination, hate speech and harassment, a suggestion was made that a "report" button should be available on the landing page of the university's website to allow staff and students to report an incident immediately. One of the drafting team members thought that this "would be a terrible idea". When we conducted empirical research on the effectiveness of the equality courts some years ago, the clerk at the Ladysmith equality court told us that limited marketing had been done for fear of the equality courts being "abused". The Bela-Bela equality court clerk indicated that people who were aware of the Act seemed to misunderstand its

4 Compare *Le Roux v Dey* 2011 3 SA 274 (CC) para 26 where the South African Constitutional Court affirmed the Supreme Court of Appeal finding that a successful claim in defamation precludes a claim based on insult, and the other way around.

purpose and approached the equality court for the "smallest things". In these anecdotes, there is an implicit argument that we should not concern equality/diversity tribunals/courts with small matters – that we should screen these matters out before they even arrive at the tribunal/court.

We argue that we should rather err in the opposite direction, and allow full hearings into life's small indignities as well – so be it a university's transformation office or an equality court/tribunal, rather hear the full argument from both parties and produce a reasoned judgment, to account to the citizenry, and to allow for some radiating effect of the court's judgment into society's *mores*.

We should add that many socio-legal scholars are sceptical about the law's ability to steer human attitudes.[5] We take a pragmatic approach. At least some complainants will be resilient and resourced enough to take legal action to vindicate their rights, to "send a message", to allow a court to deliver a pro-inclusion and pro-diversity judgment, and to allow for the possibility that the recalcitrant offender will see the error of their ways, to repent, to apologise, and to mend their ways. If "hearts and minds" legislation is passed, the (symbolic) message contained in these laws may reach some members of the populace and may lead to at least some changes in behaviour, if not their hearts. We accept that a law-induced "hearts and minds" project will not have immediate effects, and may never fully succeed, but that is not a reason to abandon such projects all together. Other social disciplines, such as education, religious studies, and sociology, should be included in research projects on how a populace's "hearts and minds" may be steered in a pro-inclusion and pro-diversity direction. If there are objections to these kinds of "Big Brother brainwashing" projects, the question that opponents would have to answer is why bigotry, homophobia, racism, sexism, xenophobia and the like should be tolerated.

We undertook a comparative survey of a number of jurisdictions' court cases and legislation concerning *de minimis* (Germany, Canada, New Zealand, The Netherlands, and Namibia), but there is a strong focus on the South African experience in this book. South Africa's history is one of large-scale state oppression, marginalisation and violence, but also one of daily, "small" humiliations suffered by the majority black population. It would be instructive to reflect on how the post-1994 South African parliament and courts responded to this history – which role has state law (legislation and courts) been playing to address past and ongoing "small" humiliations, and what could have been done better?

5 See Kok (2008), and Böcker (2020) 3 *Erasmus Law Review* 21 for an overview and discussion of this socio-legal scholarship.

We proceed as follows. In the next chapter, we consider how "triviality" has featured as a defence in courts in various jurisdictions. We list some examples from South Africa's equality courts where small slights have led to remedies being awarded to complainants. We then consider how national laws in Germany, Canada, New Zealand, The Netherlands, and Namibia address discrimination, hate speech and harassment and how these jurisdictions deal with "small" infractions. We focus in more depth on the South African approach in the next chapter. We analyse a judgment by the Constitutional Court that has hurt Parliament's "hearts and minds" project as concretised in the South African Equality Act and propose a way forward for the South African Parliament to respond to the Constitutional Court judgment. In the final chapter, we propose two ways forward for national "hearts and minds" projects that also target "small" insults. Many national highest courts give primacy to freedom of expression and have held unconstitutional attempts to outlaw merely offensive speech or conduct. Unless these courts can be persuaded to prioritise dignity, kindness, and substantive equality above freedom of expression, the second option explored in the final chapter seems more viable – create a statutory duty for state and private actors to develop and publish equality plans, and be held accountable if they do not adhere to these plans.

CHAPTER 4

The Recognition and Application of *de minimis non curat lex* in Different Jurisdictions

In this chapter, we first consider a number of general principles that seem to apply to the application of the *de minimis* maxim across jurisdictions. We then consider the application of the maxim where constitutional rights are at stake. Thirdly, we consider examples from the South African equality courts where the maxim may have come into play.

1 General Principles: Five Factors Invoked

The maxim *de minimis non curat lex* is often applied in cases perceived as raising extreme triviality, as in the case of *R v Dane*,[1] where the injury in question was the trimming of a hedge between two neighbours. Holmes J describes the situation as making "a mountain out of a mole-hill".[2] The rule expounds that the law does not concern itself with trifles. The basic meaning of the term is accordingly that the law will not resolve petty or unimportant disputes.[3] It is surprising that there has not been much focus on the relevance of this maxim as a defence to legal violations and the circumstances under which it should be applied.[4] The maxim is said to have a long but largely undeveloped history, and courts use it with little explanation or guidelines for future cases.[5] It is often applied, but seldom rationalised.[6] A possible explanation is that, since these matters are (perceived to be) by nature unimportant or insignificant, courts dismiss these claims without comprehensive reasoning.[7]

When deciding whether the maxim applies in a particular instance, it will depend upon the circumstances and facts of each case.[8] Five different fac-

1 1957 2 SA 472 (N).
2 Ibid 473.
3 Inest (2006) 21 *Berkeley Technology Law Journal* 945 948.
4 Ibid 949.
5 Brown (2013) 82 *Mississippi Law Journal* 1097 1124, 1126.
6 Veech & Moon (1947) 45 *Michigan Law Review* 537.
7 Inest (2006) 21 *Berkeley Technology Law Journal* 945 949–950.
8 *R v Maguire* 1964 4 SA 191 (RA) 193.

 | HTTPS://DOI.ORG/10.1163/9789004757523-005

tors may be identified that are invoked by courts to provide guidance when a defence of *de minimis* is considered.

1.1 First Factor: Size and Type of Harm

The first factor usually considered is the size of the harm and the type of harm.[9] The extent, duration and frequency of the infringement appear to be relevant in evaluating the position.[10] Even though small monetary damages are not sufficient to guarantee a *de minimis* holding,[11] monetary terms are often used to establish value.[12]

1.2 Second Factor: Speedy Justice

The second factor considered is practicality, the promotion of the practical and speedy promotion of justice, together with the cost of adjudication and convenience.[13] One needs to determine whether the matter will be an absurd waste of the resources of the court,[14] since each litigant who improperly seeks relief for a petty claim forces other litigants with more serious claims to await their day in court.[15] Snyman opines that the *de minimis* defence should only be allowed on the basis of practicality and the workload of the courts.[16] This factor also does not independently justify a *de minimis* ruling and is usually considered in conjunction with the purpose or objective of the particular rule.[17]

---

9 Inest (2006) 21 *Berkeley Technology Law Journal* 945 951; and Veech & Moon (1947) 45 *Michigan Law Review* 537 558.

10 *Benoni Town Council v Meyer & Others* 1961 3 SA 316 (W) 325.

11 Inest (2006) 21 *Berkeley Technology Law Journal* 945 951.

12 As an example, see *S v Kgogong* 1980 3 SA 600 (A), the leading South African case dealing with *de minimis*. The trial court held that the theft of a piece of paper was a trivial matter and that, because of the *de minimis* rule the offence must be regarded as not having been committed. On appeal the (then) Appellate Division found that the court *a quo* had erred in this finding and held that: "[T]he value of this note was [not] so negligible or that the circumstances under which it was taken are [not] so trivial that the *de minimis* rule should be applied." The conviction and sentence were consequently set aside. However also see *R v Perry* (1845) 169 ER 154 where the accused was found guilty of theft for stealing a piece of paper worth one penny.

13 Hoctor (2012) 80 *e-Mantshi* 9 13; Inest (2006) 21 *Berkeley Technology Law Journal* 945 953; McKean (1926–1927) 75 *University of Pennsylvania Law Review* 429; and Veech & Moon (1947) 45 *Michigan Law Review* 537 551.

14 *Harris v Time* 191 Cal.App.3d 449 (1987) 458.

15 *Raymon v Alvord Independent School District et al* 639 F.2d 257 (1981).

16 Snyman (2002) *Journal of South African Law* 139 141.

17 Veech & Moon (1947) 45 *Michigan Law Review* 537 551.

1.3 Third Factor: Purposive Interpretation

The third factor considered is the purpose or objective of the particular statutory or common law rule and whether application of the maxim would give rise to injustice. Some writers regard this as the most important factor[18] and say that a court, when deciding whether the maxim should apply, should only consider the harms that the rule in question is supposed to prevent.[19] Trifles are measured in terms of the purpose behind the rule of law sought to be interpreted and in terms of the injustice that may be done by application of the *de minimis* rule.[20] As Eveleigh J stated in *Gill and Another v El Vino Co Ltd*: "I find it very difficult to invoke the maxim de minimis non curat lex in a situation where that which has been denied to the plaintiff is the very thing that Parliament seeks to provide, namely facilities and services on an equal basis".[21]

1.4 Fourth Factor: Perpetrator's Intent

Another factor considered is that of intent.[22] The presence or absence of intent is regarded as indicative of whether the particular actions were reasonable or not.[23] Some courts opine that intentionally wrongful conduct should not be condoned under any circumstances.[24] Others, however, consider the intent of the wrongdoer as one of several factors and not as an absolute bar to *de minimis*.[25]

1.5 Fifth Factor: Effect on Third Parties

The final factor considered is the effect of adjudication on the rights of third parties. When adjudication will have a significant effect on third parties, courts may choose to adjudicate even though the matter, if considered in isolation,

18 Ibid 545.

19 Inest (2006) 21 *Berkeley Technology Law Journal* 945 954.

20 Veech & Moon (1947) 45 *Michigan Law Review* 537 551.

21 1983 1 All ER 398 at 402. A barman in London refused to serve women at the bar and told them that they could only be served while sitting at a table. Men were however allowed to order drinks while standing at the bar. The plaintiffs claim that they had been unlawfully discriminated against on the ground of their sex in that they were treated less favourably than men.

22 Veech & Moon (1947) 45 *Michigan Law Review* 537 551; Inest (2006) 21 *Berkeley Technology Law Journal* 945 955.

23 Hoctor (2012) 80 *e-Mantshi* 9 13.

24 Inest (2006) 21 *Berkeley Technology Law Journal* 945 955.

25 Veech & Moon (1947) 45 *Michigan Law Review* 537 554–556.

would qualify for *de minimis* treatment.[26] Snyman argues that *de minimis* should be restricted to cases where neither the individual, nor the society in general has suffered any prejudice.[27] It is also clear from *S v Visagie*[28] that the interests of the community should be taken into account when deciding whether or not the maxim should be applied. Courts often consider this factor in cases where the constitutionality of a law is argued or where important issues of statutory interpretation are debated.[29] *De minimis* also does not typically apply to class actions, even though the interest of the lead plaintiff is sometimes not very significant.[30]

2 Raising *de minimis non curat lex* in the Light of Constitutional Rights

Courts across the world disagree on whether the *de minimis* principle is applicable in the area of constitutional rights.[31] It does, however, seem as though most jurisdictions do not apply this maxim in instances where constitutional matters are considered. The United States Fifth Circuit Court of Appeals held in *Lewis v Woods* that a violation of constitutional rights is never *de minimis* and explained that by making the deprivation of such rights actionable, the law recognises the importance to society that these rights be meticulously observed.[32] In *Hessel v O'Hearn*,[33] the United States Seventh Circuit Court of Appeals noted that any violation of substantive constitutional rights entitles a prevailing plaintiff to at least nominal damages and that even the smallest

---

26 Inest (2006) 21 *Berkeley Technology Law Journal* 945 954.

27 Snyman (1975) 92 *South African Law Journal* 372 373.

28 2009 2 SACR 70 (W). In the trial court the appellant was convicted of common assault. The charge arose from an incident in which the complainant and the appellant had become involved in a verbal argument concerning repairs to the appellant's vehicle. The appellant pushed the complainant, causing him to trip over a piece of equipment and break his wrist. The appeal was based, *inter alia*, on the ground that the magistrate ought to have applied *de minimis non curat lex*. The appeal was successful and the conviction and sentence were set aside.

29 Inest (2006) 21 *Berkeley Technology Law Journal* 945 954. See for example *Ballin v Los Angeles County Fair* 43 Cal.App.2d Supp. 884 (1941).

30 Nemerofsky (2001–2002) 37 *Gonzaga Law Review* 315. See also Sasso (2004–2005) 31 *Litigation* 16.

31 Nemerofsky (2001–2002) 37 *Gonzaga Law Review* 315 331.

32 *Lewis v Woods* 848 F.2d 649 (5th Cir. 1988). In *Pulman Co v Dudley* 77 S.W.2d 592, 593 (Tex. Civ. App. 1934) the court also made the statement that *de minimis* is not applicable if a substantial right has been violated.

33 977 F.2d 299 (7th Cir. 1992) 301–304.

intrusions are actionable. State courts in California,[34] Florida,[35] Pennsylvania,[36] Iowa[37] and Maryland[38] have specifically stated that any gender-based price discrimination, regardless of severity or motivation, is illegal, while the New Jersey legislature drafted a bill that includes a *de minimis* defence where the contention is made that ladies' nights are discriminatory towards men.[39] The attempts to amend the New Jersey civil rights laws to allow ladies' nights failed.[40] In *Ladd v Iowa West Racing Association*,[41] the Iowa Supreme Court held that a racetrack's denial of free admission to a male customer on Ladies Day violated Iowa's Civil Rights Act.

De minimis can be raised for a variety of reasons, one being that the matter is an "isolated incident". Legislation however does not establish isolatedness as deserving judicial rejection and some commentators are even of the opinion that the term should be removed from constitutional jurisprudence altogether.[42] Another ground often listed is that the incident is "bad, but not bad enough".[43] For both of these grounds, it is difficult to establish where the line should be drawn.[44] How many incidents are required for something not to be "isolated" or how bad is "bad enough"? If these rights really matter and are classified as "fundamental", then a violation of any size should be regarded as significant.[45]

Considering the factors of the time and cost of adjudication and the goal of the promotion of practical and speedy administration of justice,[46] some commentators are of the opinion that present convenience or expediency can never justify the slightest disregard of a constitutional provision.[47] Supreme Court Justice O'Connor's concurrence in *Elk Grove Unified School District v*

34 *Koire v Metro Car Wash* 707 P.2d 195 203–204 (1985).

35 *City of Clearwater v. Studebaker's Dance Club* 516 So.2d 1106 (Fla. Dist. Ct. App. 1987).

36 *Pennsylvania Liquor Control Board v. Dobrinoff* 471 A.2d 941 (1984).

37 *Ladd v Iowa West Racing Ass'n* 438 N.W.2d 600 (Iowa 1989).

38 *Peppin v Woodside Delicatessen* 506 A.2d 263 (Md. Ct. Spec. App. 1986).

39 Rank (2005–2006) 36 *Seton Hall Law Review* 223 226.

40 Ford (2011) *Slate.*

41 443 N.W.2d 600 (Iowa 1989).

42 Bernstein (2010) 62 *Florida Law Review* 895 924. In *S v Steenberg* 1999 1 SACR 594 (N) a single incident of racial name calling was sufficient to find the defendant guilty of *crimen iniuria*. The court found that such utterances could not be regarded as trivial. See also *S v Mostert* 2006 1 SACR 560 (N).

43 Bernstein (2010) 62 *Florida Law Review* 895 925.

44 White (1998) 47 *Emory Law Journal* 1121 1129.

45 Bernstein (2010) 62 *Florida Law Review* 895 948.

46 Hoctor (2012) 80 *e-Mantshi* 9 13; Snyman (2002) *Journal of South African Law* 139 141.

47 Guthrie (1898) 40.

Newdow[48] included a noteworthy statement concerning *de minimis*. The judge suggested that "[t]here are no *de minimis* violations of the Constitution – no constitutional harms so slight that the courts are obliged to ignore them".[49]

The applicability of this maxim in constitutional matters has been questioned and disputed for many years. Consider for example the opinion of Guthrie as stated in his lectures on the fourteenth article of amendment to the Constitution of the United States:[50]

> There is another rule in construing or expounding a constitution, and that is that the ancient maxim "*de minimis non curat lex*" has no application. The violation of a constitutional right should never be measured or met by any such plea.

Guthrie also refers to the case of US Supreme Court case of *Sentell v New Orleans & Carrollton Railroad Company*,[51] where counsel attempted to argue that the invasion of constitutional rights in the particular instance was slight. Counsel was, however, firmly reminded that the case involved the Constitution of the United States and that the degree or extent of the invasion was irrelevant. Guthrie further explains that moderation is no justification for keeping silent when a constitutional right is invaded and that there is "no greater political blindness, no more dangerous policy" than the sanctioning of constitutional infringements merely because the particular instance seems harmless.[52] When justiciable rights in a Bill of Rights are adjudicated, judges should not be misled by the seemingly trifle facts – they should set their aim at the underlying principal issues.[53]

48 542 U.S. 1 (2004).

49 *Elk Grove Unified School District v Newdow* 542 US 1 (2004) 37.

50 Guthrie (1898) 39–40.

51 *Sentell v New Orleans & Carrollton Railroad Company* 166 U.S. 698 (1897). This case concerned the constitutionality of a law of Louisiana requiring dogs to be placed on assessment rolls and limiting any recovery by an owner to the value fixed by himself for the purpose of taxation.

52 Guthrie (1898) 40.

53 See Karst (1974) 35 *Ohio State Law Journal* 546 for an analysis of a court case where the court dismissed a petition to register as "Ms" to vote while the applicable legislation at the time forced women to register either as "Miss" or "Mrs". This complaint was explicitly referred to as trivial by one of the presiding judges. Also see Newman (1998) 28 *Cumberland Law Review* 1 6 who seem to argue that a complaint based on the USA coins saying "in God we trust" and the crier in the US Supreme Court intoning "God save the United States and this honourable Court" should be met by *de minimis non curat lex*.

3 Examples of High Court Judgments of South African Equality Courts

The South African Equality Act expresses the need to take measures at all levels to eliminate discrimination and inequalities.[54] The success or failure of the legislative prohibitions in the Act depends on the mechanisms of enforcement and actual application of the prohibitions.[55] If one considers the reported judgments of South African equality courts at High Court level,[56] none of these cases dealt with a complaint that could by any stretch of the imagination be thought of as trivial – except perhaps a judgment that related to a high school that prohibited a Hindu learner from wearing a small nose stud in school.[57] In the event, this "small" violation proceeded to the South African Constitutional Court, where the Court could use this "small" infraction to, for the first time, provide its interpretation of section 14 of the Equality Act and make important pronouncements on the value of diversity in South African schools.[58] All of the other reported High Court judgments reflect serious instances of discrimination or hate speech:

- a cartoon depicting hate speech against homosexuals;[59]
- a song containing the phrase "shoot the boer";[60]
- a speech by a politician making light of women's experience of rape;[61]
- a decision by the Dutch Reformed Church Synod to disallow same sex couples to marry in the church;[62]
- a decision to curtail artisanal fishing rights;[63]

54 Sec 4(2)(b).

55 Kruger (2011) 7 *The Equal Rights Review* 27 29.

56 In South Africa, High Court judgments are in principle binding precedent, whether reported (published) in the law reports or not.

57 *Pillay v MEC for Education, KwaZulu-Natal, and Others* 2006 6 SA 363 (EqC); *Pillay v MEC for Education, KwaZulu-Natal, and Others* 2006 10 BCLR 1237 (N).

58 *MEC for Education: Kwazulu-Natal and Others v Pillay* 2007 2 SA 106 (CC).

59 *South African Human Rights Commission v Qwelane* (44/EQJHB) [2011] ZAEQC. The cartoon was accompanied by an article that asserted that homosexuality was wrong and that the sections in the South African Constitution that gives license to men marrying men should be removed before some idiot demands to marry an animal.

60 *Afri-Forum and Another v Malema and Others* (20968/2010) [2011] ZAEQC. The literal meaning of the word "boer" in South Africa is generally understood to be a reference to white Afrikaans-speaking males.

61 *Sonke Gender Justice Network v Malema* 2010 7 BCLR 729 (EqC).

62 *Gaum and Others v Van Rensburg NO and Others* [2019] 2 All SA 722 (GP).

63 *Minister of Environmental Affairs and Tourism v George and Others* 2007 3 SA 62 (SCA).

- allegations of unfair discrimination based on race in the horse racing industry;[64]
- allegations of unfair discrimination based on race in the shortlisting and appointment of applicants as regional magistrates;[65]
- a gay music teacher being fired when his sexual orientation became known to the church where he provided music lessons;[66]
- allegations of unfair discrimination based on race in the submissions of tenders for the construction of provincial roads;[67]
- a vision-impaired Indian female denied appointment as a magistrate;[68]
- a white man insulting a black man as a "baboon";[69]
- an allegation of gender-based discrimination and abuse of corporate power in a rape case;[70]
- the use of the "k word";[71]
- an argument that the Equality Act should be published in all eleven official languages (at that point, the Act had not been published in all official languages);[72]
- the differential treatment of prisoners in different prisons;[73]
- an allegation of hate speech towards supporters of the state of Israel;[74]
- an allegation of hate speech against a person who stated on social media that "we must act against whites as Hitler did to the Jews";[75] and

---

64 *Maharaj v National Horseracing Authority of Southern Africa* 2008 4 SA 59 (N).

65 *Du Preez v The Minister of Justice and Constitutional Development* 2006 5 SA 592 (EqC).

66 *Strydom v Nederduitse Gereformeerde Gemeente Moreleta Park* [2008] ZAGPHC 269; (2009) 30 ILJ 868 (EqC).

67 *Manong and Associates (Pty) Ltd v Eastern Cape Department of Roads and Transport & Others* 2009 6 SA 589 (SCA).

68 *Singh v Minister of Justice and Constitutional Development and Others* 2013 3 SA 66 (EqC).

69 *Strydom v Chiloane* 2008 2 SA 247 (T); and also see *Herselman v Geleba* (231/2009) [2011] ZAECGHC 108.

70 *S v Neotel (Pty) Ltd* 2019 1 SA 622 (GJ).

71 *Thembani v Swanepoel* 2017 3 SA 70 (ECM). The deplorable word "kaffer" in Afrikaans or "kaffir" in South African English is comparable to the use of the word "nigger" in the United States.

72 *Lourens v Speaker of the National Assembly of Parliament and Others* [2016] 2 All SA 340 (SCA).

73 *Pretorius and Others v Minister of Justice and Correctional Services and Others* 2018 2 SACR 501 (GP).

74 *SAHRC obo South African Jewish Board of Deputies v Masuku and Another* 2018 3 SA 291 (GJ) and on appeal to the Supreme Court of Appeal *Masuku and Another v South African Human Rights Commission obo South African Jewish Board of Deputies* 2019 2 SA 194 (SCA).

75 *South African Human Rights Commission v Khumalo* 2019 1 SA 289 (GJ).

- and an allegation of unfair discrimination based on ethnic origin and nationality against the police for failing to act against xenophobic violence.[76]

No cases dealing with harassment were reported in High Court equality court matters.

4 A Survey Sample of Lower Court Judgments in South African Equality Courts 2008–2012

At the lower court level,[77] South African equality courts have from time to time dealt with matters that some commentators would probably describe as "isolated events" or instances that are "bad, but not bad enough". Complainants in High Court equality court matters would probably employ lawyers as these matters are more likely to be high-stakes, complex disputes. Lower court equality court matters are probably more often utilised by complainants who are not represented by lawyers and are probably easier to resolve one way or the other. It may then also be assumed that these cases are more likely to be seen as unmeritorious than High Court equality court cases, or that it may be argued that courts are not the most appropriate forums to have these kinds of disputes resolved.

With the assistance of law students as researchers, we collated equality court files from a number of lower equality courts for the period roughly from 2008 to 2012, to get a better sense of "living" South African equality law. The vast majority of equality court disputes are being heard in these lower courts, yet no central database exists to gauge the nature of complaints being lodged in these courts and the outcomes of these cases. We present only a small sample of cases here, to give the reader some sense of the categories of cases and how *de minimis non curat lex* could potentially operate at the lower court level.

Reflecting on the sample of cases used here, a number of distinctions can be drawn:

a) Serious incidents that are not reflected in the remedy awarded;
b) Incidents that do not meet the requirements set out in the Equality Act for discrimination, hate speech and harassment and are dismissed;
c) Incidents where the qualifiers ("unfair", "persistent" or "serious", "harmful" or "hurtful") are not carefully and context-sensitively applied;

76 *Osman v Minister of Safety and Security and Others* (EC09/2008) [2010] ZAEQC 1.

77 Lower court judgments do not form binding precedent in South Africa. These judgments are not reported anywhere. A researcher interested in these findings would have to travel to the specific lower court and draw the relevant hard copy file from the filing office.

d) Incidents where the correct cause of action is identified and an appropriate remedy granted; and
e) Incidents that meet all the requirements for one or more of the causes of action but that are dismissed for being too trivial to warrant a court's attention.

(It should also be noted that the judgments surveyed here were handed down prior to the Constitutional Court striking the qualifier "hurtful" from the definition of hate speech. This decision is subjected to stringent criticism in 6.2.4 (d) below.)

Here are a few examples from each of these categories.

(a) Serious incidents that are not reflected in the remedy awarded
- Use of the "k" word – the equality court found that unfair discrimination occurred and ordered that a conference take place with the manager to work out rules of conduct between the parties.[78]
- The respondent used the "k" word and slapped the respondent – the court ordered that an apology be made towards the complainant and payment of R2000 compensation.[79]
- Use of the "k" word – the court ordered payment of R6585 and issued a peace order.[80]
- Neighbourly dispute where one neighbour shouts to the other "fuck off Jews", "fucking kikes", "you should all go to the gas chambers and burn, burn, burn" – court ordered an apology to be made.[81]
- Respondent calls the complainant a "mooi kaffermeisie" or "mooi kaffermeidjie"[82] – complaint dismissed because court held that respondent did not intend to defame the complainant.[83]
- Use of the "k" word – respondent ordered to apologise.[84]
- The complainant alleged that the respondent had called her a bitch, the "k" word and prostitute in front of a colleague – respondent ordered to apologise.[85]

The Equality Act introduces the unconditional apology as a remedy. This remedy is not completely unknown in South Africa though, since the common

78 Benoni equality court case numbers 2009/1, 2009/2, 2009/3.
79 Benoni equality court case number 2012/12.
80 Boksburg equality court case number 2013/5A.
81 Cape Town equality court case number 2008/2.
82 Roughly translated as "pretty kaffir girl".
83 Cape Town equality court case number 2008/8.
84 Belfast equality court case number 2007/6.
85 Durban equality court case number 2004/22.

law of delict also presented *amende honorable* as a remedy that consisted of a declaration and apology for an infringement. Constitutional Court judges have also commented favourably on this remedy in such instances.[86] It may be asked if a court-ordered apology is sufficient when vile insults such as the "k" word is used.

(b) Incidents that do not meet the requirements set out in the Equality Act for discrimination, hate speech and harassment and are dismissed.

For the examples below, either the impugned expression was not based on a prohibited ground, or the impugned statement was not insulting:

- The respondent alleged that the complainant stole money – the case was correctly dismissed.[87]
- The respondent alleged that the complainant bewitched them – the case was correctly dismissed.[88]
- The respondent alleged that the complainant was HIV positive – cases correctly dismissed.[89]
- The respondent alleged that the complainant was HIV positive and had an abortion – the case was correctly dismissed.[90]
- The respondent alleged that the complainant was a murderer – the case was correctly dismissed.[91]
- The respondent said to the complainant, "your boyfriend is dead from your disease" – the case was correctly dismissed.[92]

(c) Incidents where the qualifiers ("unfair", "persistent", "serious", "hurtful", "based on a prohibited ground") are not carefully and context-sensitively applied:

- The respondent alleged that the complainant had AIDS, called them a bitch and that they gave up a child for adoption – complaint wrongly dismissed.[93]

---

86 *Le Roux v Dey* 2011 3 SA 274 (CC) 333–336.

87 Benoni equality court case number 2010/4 and case number 2013/3; Boksburg equality court case number 2013/4 and 2013/5.

88 Benoni equality court case number 2011/3 and for similar allegation Germiston equality court case number 2013/10.

89 Benoni equality court case number 2012/9 and case number 2013/8.

90 Benoni equality court case number 2013/7.

91 Boksburg equality court case number 2012/1.

92 Boksburg equality court case number 2013/3.

93 Benoni equality court case number 2013/4. Calling a woman a "bitch" is insulting based on the prohibited grounds of sex and gender. Post-*Qwelane* this claim would have to be brought in terms of the common law *actio iniuriarum*.

- The respondent called the complainant a slave and a fool – complaint wrongly dismissed and referred to another forum.[94]
- The respondent called the complainant a bitch and slut – complaint wrongly dismissed (and suggested to complainant to institute criminal proceedings).[95]
- The respondent called the complainant a bitch who sleep with married men – complaint wrongly dismissed.[96]
- The respondent called the complainant a witch and alleged that they were HIV positive – the complainant was incorrectly upheld; R1500 awarded in damages and the respondent ordered to apologise.[97]
- The respondent told the complainant that her husband died of AIDS – complaint wrongly upheld; respondent ordered to apologise to the complainant.[98]
- The respondent told the complainant that they have AIDS – wrongly ordered to apologise and to pay R300 to the Khanya frail care centre.[99]
- The respondent called the complainant a dog, stupid, and a bitch – wrongly dismissed and referred to civil court.[100]

(d) Incidents where the correct cause of action is identified and an appropriate remedy granted:
- School ordered to make the necessary adjustments so that the school is accessible to a learner in a wheelchair.[101]

---

94 Boksburg equality court case number 2013/1. Calling a black male a "slave" is arguably insulting based on the prohibited ground of race.

95 Boksburg equality court case number 2013/6. Calling a woman a "bitch" and a "slut" is insulting based on the prohibited grounds of sex and gender. Post-*Qwelane* this claim would have to be brought in terms of the common law *actio iniuriarum*.

96 Germiston equality court case number 2013/9. See the explanation directly above.

97 Seemingly the only case decided in the Barberton equality court in 2010. Unless it is suggested that calling someone a "witch" is insulting based on the prohibited grounds of conscience and belief, it is not clear how a finding of hate speech was made on this expression. Arguably courts have a public education duty too, to pronounce that belief in witchcraft is irrational. The same would go for alleging that someone is HIV positive or has AIDS. No stigma should attach to a person based on their HIV/AIDS status.

98 Belfast equality court case number 2007/4. See the explanation directly above.

99 Belfast equality court case 2011. See the explanation above on HIV/AIDS status.

100 Witbank equality court case number 2007/3. See the explanation above on the "bitch" slur.

101 Witbank equality court case number 2010/1. If a school is inaccessible to a disabled learner, that would be systemic unfair discrimination and should be remedied by an intrusive remedy as ordered in this case.

- Dispute in a sectional title housing complex between a member of the board of trustees and one of the residents; a resident called the trustee an "old cripple" – meeting of the body corporate called where the resident had to apologise.[102]

(e) Incidents that meet all the requirements for one or more of the causes of action but that are dismissed for being too trivial to warrant a court's attention.

Where equality courts dismiss cases, the reason usually provided is that the wrong forum was chosen for the particular dispute – not that the dispute was too small to be entertained by a court.

The overall picture that emerges from this comparative overview is that, for the most part, courts are willing to consider "trivial" infringements where constitutional rights – such as the complainant's dignity – are implicated.

102 Roodepoort equality court case number 2009/6. Referring to a disabled person as "cripple" is insulting. Post-*Qwelane* this claim would have to be based on the common law *actio iniuriarum*.

CHAPTER 5

A National Comparative Survey of the *de minimis* Defence

This chapter provides a snapshot of legislation from various jurisdictions where these laws could in principle be used to address micro-aggressions, namely Germany, Canada, New Zealand, the Netherlands and Namibia. These countries either receive a large number of migrants or have a history of genocide or the oppression of indigenous populations. We describe their legislative frameworks and then their broader anti-discrimination policies to determine whether or not they are designed to address micro-aggressions.

1 Germany

1.1 Germany's Anti-discrimination Law

Germany's primary anti-discrimination legislation is the General Act on Equal Treatment.[1] The European Commission has been conducting and publishing annual comparative analysis reports on the non-discrimination laws in all of the European Union's member states,[2] as well as reports on developing anti-discrimination laws in the member states since 2005.[3] Germany's General Act on Equal Treatment, which was promulgated in 2006, was later amended in 2022 to align with the anti-discrimination law requirements issued by the European Commission in its reports. The purpose of the General Act on Equal Treatment is to prevent discrimination on the grounds of race or ethnic origin, gender, religion or belief, disability, age or sexual orientation.[4] German law recognises both direct and indirect forms of discrimination.[5] However, in

1 General Act on Equal Treatment of 14 August 2006 (Federal Law Gazette I, p. 1897), as last amended by Article 4 of the Act of 19 December 2022 (Federal Law Gazette I, p. 2510).

2 See Publications Office of the European Union at https://op.europa.eu/en/home (accessed on 31 May 2025).

3 Bell & Cormack (2005).

4 Sec 1 of Germany's General Act on Equal Treatment.

5 Sec 3: "1) Direct discrimination is taken to occur where one person is treated less favourably than another is, has been or would be treated in a comparable situation on any of the grounds referred to in section 1. Direct discrimination on the ground of gender is also taken

 | HTTPS://DOI.ORG/10.1163/9789004757523-006

section 2, the Act quite narrowly defines the scope of its application to include only conditions for access to dependent employment and self-employment, employment conditions and working conditions, access to vocational guidance and training, membership of a workers' and employers' organisation, social protection, social advantages, education, and access to and the supply of goods and services.[6] German law, therefore, limits discriminatory acts to conduct practised in particular places and in particular instances. A discriminatory act that falls outside of the scope outlined in section 2 is not sanctionable in terms of the Act.

An example of a discriminatory act falling outside of the scope of section 2 is a customer at a grocery store who refuses to be served by a teller wearing a hijab. This conduct, which is a display of less favourable treatment (in terms of the Act) by the customer towards the teller on the grounds of religion and/or race, would not be sanctionable in terms of the Act, as the discriminatory conduct does not fall within the scope of section 2. In this example, although the teller is at work, the customer is neither her employer nor a fellow employee. Additionally, the customer is the recipient of a service, and the teller is the provider thereof. So, although the teller was the subject of differential treatment, it cannot be said that she suffered a disadvantage as a result of the discriminatory practice, and therefore it is not discrimination as recognised by the General Act on Equal Treatment, although it would quite easily classify as a micro-aggression.

---

to occur in relation to section 2 (1) nos. 1 to 4 in the event of the less favourable treatment of a woman on account of pregnancy or maternity. 2) Indirect discrimination is taken to occur where an apparently neutral provision, criterion or practice is liable to put persons at a particular disadvantage compared with other persons on any of the grounds referred to in section 1, unless that provision, criterion or practice is objectively justified by a legitimate aim and the means of achieving that aim are appropriate and necessary".

6 Sec 2: "1) For the purposes of this Act, discrimination on any of the grounds referred to in section 1 is impermissible in relation to: 1. conditions for access to dependent employment and self-employment, including selection criteria and recruitment conditions, whatever the branch of activity and at all levels of the professional hierarchy, including promotion, 2. employment conditions and working conditions, including pay and reasons for dismissal, in particular in contracts between individuals, collective bargaining agreements and measures to implement and terminate an employment relationship, as well as for promotion, 3. access to all types and to all levels of vocational guidance, vocational training, advanced vocational training and retraining, including practical work experience, 4. membership of and involvement in an organisation of workers or employers or any other organisation whose members carry on a particular profession, including the benefits provided for by such organisations, 5. social protection, including social security and health care, 6. social advantages, 7. education, 8. access to and supply of goods and services which are available to the public, including housing".

Furthermore, in the case of a micro-invalidation, and even micro-insults that fall within the ambit of section 2 of the Act, if there is no comparable disadvantage suffered by a person the micro-aggression would not fit the definitions of either direct or indirect discrimination in terms of section 3 of the Act.

1.2 Germany's Legal Treatment of Harassment

Section 3 of the General Act on Equal Treatment identifies and defines three additional forms of discrimination, namely harassment, sexual harassment and instruction to discriminate. The most applicable one, for our purposes, is harassment, which reads:

> Harassment is deemed to be discrimination when unwanted conduct in connection with any of the grounds referred to in section 1 takes place with the purpose or effect of violating the dignity of the person concerned and of creating an intimidating, hostile, degrading, humiliating or offensive environment.[7]

The application of the above provision has been interpreted by German Labour Courts in the following manner:

> What is essential for harassment within the meaning of Section 3 Paragraph 3 of the General Act on Equal Treatment is the violation of a person's dignity, which is intended or brought about by the undesirable behaviour, as well as the creation of a hostile environment. The last clause of Section 3 Paragraph 3 of the General Act on Equal Treatment explicitly focuses on whether an environment characterized by 'intimidation, hostility, degradation, humiliation or insults' is created. The legal wording thus lists particularly serious examples of behaviour that violates dignity, which must necessarily be present in addition to the violation of dignity.[8]

In the aforementioned case, the Labour Court was tasked with adjudicating an allegation of harassment on the grounds of race by a Croatian employee who was repeatedly required by her employer to take German language lessons in order to communicate with clients. In that case, the Court held that, although requiring a sufficient command of the German language as a condition for employment might constitute indirect discrimination on the grounds

7 Sec 3(3) of the Act.
8 LAG Schleswig-Holstein, judgment of 23.12.2009, 6 Sa 158/09 10.

of ethnic origin, because the majority of those adversely affected would not be of German origin, the requirement was justified in that particular case.[9]

The requirement by German Courts that the behaviour violating another's dignity be "serious", coupled with the creation of an outwardly hostile environment, would make it difficult to prosecute micro-aggressions, which are not likely to be viewed as "serious" behaviours by courts.

1.3 The German Law on Public Order and the Crime of Incitement

A disturbance of the public peace,[10] and the dissemination of content that is hateful or that incites violence,[11] is criminalised in section 130 of the German Criminal Code.[12] Section 130(1), on a disturbance of the public peace, reads as follows:

> Whoever, in a manner suited to causing a disturbance of the public peace, incites hatred against a national, racial, religious group or a group defined by their ethnic origin, against sections of the population or individuals on account of their belonging to one of the aforementioned groups or sections of the population, or calls for violent or arbitrary measures against them or violates the human dignity of others by insulting, maliciously maligning or defaming one of the aforementioned groups, sections of the population or individuals on account of their belonging to one of the aforementioned groups or sections of the population incurs a penalty of imprisonment for a term of between three months and five years.

9 LAG Schleswig-Holstein, judgment of 23.12.2009, 6 Sa 158/09 9.

10 Sec 130(1) of the German Criminal Code.

11 Sec 130(2) of the German Criminal Code: "Whoever (1) disseminates content (section 11 (3)) or makes it available to the public, or offers, supplies or makes available to a person under 18 years of age content (section 11 (3)) which 1. incites hatred against one of the groups referred to in subsection (1) no. 1, sections of the population or individuals on account of their belonging to one of the groups referred to in subsection (1) no. 1, or sections of the population, 2. calls for violent or arbitrary measures against one of the persons or bodies of persons referred to in letter (a) or 3. attacks the human dignity of one of the persons or bodies of persons referred to in letter (a) by insulting, maliciously maligning or defaming them, or (2) produces, purchases, supplies, stocks, offers, advertises or undertakes to import or export content (section 11 (3)) as referred to in no. 1 (a) to (c) in order to use it within the meaning of no. 1 or to facilitate such use by another, incurs a penalty of imprisonment for a term not exceeding three years or a fine".

12 Criminal Code in the version published on 13 November 1998 (Federal Law Gazette I, p. 3322), as last amended by Article 2 of the Act of 22 November 2021 (Federal Law Gazette I, p. 4906).

Section 130(1) sets out two ways in which the crime of a disturbance of the public peace may be committed. The first is by inciting hatred or calling for violence against a protected group, and the second is by violating someone's human dignity by "insulting, maliciously maligning or defaming" such a person.

According to the German Federal Court of Justice, mere insult against a person is not enough.[13] There must be an "assault on [a person's] equal right to life in the public community, which treats [them] as an inferior being".[14] Additionally, it appears that a statement must be made, and that the statement must be "capable of disturbing the public peace". In determining whether or not a statement is capable of disturbing the public peace, the following factors are taken into consideration: the content and the intensity of the statement, the receptivity of the population, and especially of the youth, the potential for violence, and the sensitivity of the affected group.[15]

The gravity of the insult and level of disturbance to the public peace required by the German courts strongly suggests that section 130(1) of the German Criminal Code does not encompass the ability to prosecute less abrasive micro-aggressions.

1.4 Broader German Anti-discrimination Policy Frameworks

In addition to the legislative framework outlined above, Germany has, in the form of national policies, a National Action Plan Against Racism and a National Strategy Against Antisemitism and for Jewish Life.

The National Action Plan Against Racism focuses on antisemitism, anti-gypsyism, Islamophobia, racism against black people, homophobia, transphobia, and discrimination against refugees and migrants.[16] This particular national policy, in addition to the prosecution of discrimination, aims to tackle discrimination through the formal education system, through civic education and by promoting specialised training in the workplace to ensure inclusivity and a discrimination-free environment.[17]

The National Strategy Against Antisemitism and for Jewish Life is more comprehensive. This policy creates structures in which the German government and civil society actors can work together in a targeted manner. It creates action areas to prevent antisemitism by applying a broad-based approach to

13 See BGH [1994] NJW 1421 in Oxford Pro Bono Publico (2012) para 115.

14 Ibid.

15 Oxford Pro Bono Publico (2012) para 118.

16 National Action Plan Against Racism 10–12.

17 National Action Plan Against Racism 20–23 and 28–33.

combating it.[18] These action areas include data collection, research, the publication of a situation report, education, creating a culture of remembrance, applying punitive measures, and learning about Jewish history and Jewish life today.[19] The National Strategy Against Antisemitism and for Jewish Life takes into account the perspectives of those affected by antisemitism[20] and aims to penalise antisemitism even when expressed in ways that do not constitute an offence under criminal law.[21]

1.5 Conclusions as to the German Legal Framework

Because of its violently discriminatory past, Germany's legal framework is quite harsh when it comes to punishing a threat or perceived threat against the public peace and incitement of violence or hatred. However, when it comes to curbing discriminatory practices, Germany, quite curiously, limits the scope of the application of its anti-discrimination legislation, as well as the legal definitions of discriminatory conduct and practices. This means that the ability to interpret Germany's anti-discrimination legislation to include micro-aggressions is very limited.

Germany has a broader anti-discrimination framework in the form of national action plans. Its most comprehensive and developed national policy is aimed at combatting antisemitism, specifically. The policy, or action plan, is comprehensive enough to be able to address micro-aggressions, and educate against them, but only in the context of antisemitism.

2 Canada

2.1 Canada's Anti-discrimination Law

Canada's anti-discrimination legal framework is enshrined in its Constitution[22] and enabled in its Human Rights Act.[23] The Human Rights Act prohibits discrimination on the grounds of race, national or ethnic origin, colour, religion, age, sex, sexual orientation, gender identity or expression, marital status,

18 National Strategy Against Antisemitism and for Jewish Life 10.
19 National Strategy Against Antisemitism and for Jewish Life 23–44.
20 National Strategy Against Antisemitism and for Jewish Life 12–14.
21 National Strategy Against Antisemitism and for Jewish Life 37.
22 Sec 15 of Canadian Charter of Rights and Freedoms.
23 R.S.C., 1985, c. H-6.

family status, genetic characteristics, disability and conviction for an offence for which a pardon has been granted or in respect of which a record suspension has been ordered.[24]

The Canadian Human Rights Act limits discriminatory practices to the provision of goods or services, access to a facility or accommodation,[25] access to a commercial premises or residential accommodation,[26] employment,[27] employment applications and advertisements,[28] membership to an employee organisation,[29] discriminatory workplace policies or practices,[30] equal wages,[31] publication of discriminatory notices,[32] harassment[33] and sexual harassment.[34]

2.2 The Canadian Legal Treatment of Harassment

Section 14(1) of the Human Rights Act stipulates that:

> It is a discriminatory practice,
> - in the provision of goods, services, facilities or accommodation customarily available to the general public,
> - in the provision of commercial premises or residential accommodation, or
> - in matters related to employment,
>
> to harass an individual on a prohibited ground of discrimination.

"Harass" is not defined by the Act. However, the Canadian Human Rights Tribunal[35] has determined that in order to establish a *prima facie* case of discriminatory harassment it must be established that the conduct complained of was related to a prohibited ground of discrimination, was unsolicited or unwelcome, and has adverse consequences for the victim, or in the case of

24 Sec 3(1) of the Canadian Human Rights Act.
25 Sec 5 of the Canadian Human Rights Act.
26 Sec 6 of the Canadian Human Rights Act.
27 Sec 7 of the Canadian Human Rights Act.
28 Sec 8 of the Canadian Human Rights Act.
29 Sec 9 of the Canadian Human Rights Act.
30 Sec 10 of the Canadian Human Rights Act.
31 Sec 11 of the Canadian Human Rights Act.
32 Sec 12 of the Canadian Human Rights Act.
33 Sec 14(1) of the Canadian Human Rights Act.
34 Sec 14(2) of the Canadian Human Rights Act.
35 *Bilac v Abbey and Others*, 2023 CHRT 43 (CanLII) para 22; and *Nielsen v Nee Tahi Buhn Indian Band*, 2019 CHRT 50 (CanLII) paras 116–117.

employment,[36] was persistent or serious enough to create a hostile or negative work environment that undermined the complainant's dignity.

It is very clear from sections 14(1)(a) to (c) that harassment, like other discriminatory practices in the Act, is limited to the instances outlined in the subsections. Given the overtness and persistence, or "seriousness", of harassment it would be difficult to prosecute micro-aggressions in terms of this provision.

2.3 The Canadian Law on Incitement and Wilful Promotion of Hatred

Hate speech or the incitement of hatred is not covered by Canada's anti-discrimination legislation, but is rather criminalised in its Criminal Code.

In terms of section 319 of the Canadian Criminal Code, the commission of the following are criminal offences:

> Section 319(1): Everyone who, by communicating statements in any public place, incites hatred against any identifiable group where such incitement is likely to lead to a breach of the peace is guilty of an indictable offence and is liable to imprisonment for a term not exceeding two years; or an offence punishable on summary conviction.
>
> Section 319(2): Everyone who, by communicating statements, other than in private conversation, wilfully promotes hatred against any identifiable group is guilty of an indictable offence and is liable to imprisonment for a term not exceeding two years; or an offence punishable on summary conviction.

According to the Superior Court of Quebec in *Dion v R*,[37] four elements must be established in order to prove the rarely invoked offence of incitement to hatred, in terms of section 319(1) of the Criminal Code. They are as follows: The communication of statements that incite hatred; in a public place; against an identifiable group; and such incitement must be likely to lead to a breach of the peace.[38]

"Hatred" was understood by the Supreme Court of Canada in *Saskatchewan Human Rights Commission v Whatcott*[39] to be restricted to those extreme manifestations of the emotion described by the words "detestation" and "vilification".[40] This filters out expression which, while repugnant and offensive, does

36 See sec 14(1)(c) of the Canadian Human Rights Act.

37 2020 (CanLII) 3049 (QCCS).

38 *Dion v R* 2020 (CanLII) 3049 (QCCS) para 20.

39 2013 SCC 11, [2013] 1 SCR 467.

40 *Saskatchewan Human Rights Commission v Whatcott* 2013 SCC 11, [2013] 1 SCR 467 para 57.

not incite the level of abhorrence, delegitimisation and rejection that risks causing discrimination or other harmful effects.[41] The denigration must be extreme and flagrant. Therefore, "hatred" excludes statements that are only offensive and hurtful.[42] Additionally, an act can only be considered a "breach of the peace" if it involves some degree of violence and a risk of harm.[43]

It is again worth noting that the essence of micro-aggressions is their subtlety. Subtlety, by definition, does not engender the strong emotions that the Canadian system looks for in "hatred". It is therefore simple enough to conclude that micro-aggressions are precluded from prosecution under the incitement to hatred.

Separate to an incitement to hatred, a wilful promotion of hatred in contravention of section 319(2) of the Criminal Code, is proven through the establishment of the following five elements: The defendant communicated statement; the statements were communicated other than in private conversation; the statements promoted hatred; the promotion of hatred was against an identifiable group; and the defendant did so wilfully.[44]

The wording of section 319, as a whole, clearly requires an element of "public" incitement and of a "public" promotion of hatred[45] for it to amount to an offence, which would exclude micro-aggressions that predominantly take place on a one-on-one basis, and not on a public scale. Furthermore, "hatred" specifically excludes hurtful or offensive statements, which are generally the form in which micro-aggressions take place.

2.4 Canadian Broader Anti-discrimination Policy Frameworks

Although Canada has comprehensive anti-discrimination legislation, its broader policy framework aims to address systemic and institutional racism. Canada developed an anti-racism strategy, which it planned to implement over a four-year period, from 2019 to 2022.[46] Additionally, Canada released a discussion paper in 2023 on systemic racism, which recognised micro-aggressions as a form of individual, or person-to-person, racism.[47]

---

41 *Saskatchewan Human Rights Commission v Whatcott* 2013 SCC 11, [2013] 1 SCR 467 para 57.

42 *Dion v R* 2020 (CanLII) 3049 (QCCS) para 26.

43 *Dion v R* 2020 (CanLII) 3049 (QCCS) para 59.

44 *R v Harding*, 2001 (CanLII) 28036 ON SC para 7.

45 See *R v Keegstra*, 1990 (CanLII) 24 (SCC); (1990) 3 RCS 772i–773a.

46 Building a Foundation for Change: Canada's Anti-Racism Strategy 2019–2022, Catalogue no. CH37-4/29-2019E, ISBN 978-0-660-31004-6.

47 Discussion paper on systemic racism in 2023, Cat. No.: HR4-100/2023E-PDF, ISSN: 978-0-660-49407-4 6.

The discussion paper also suggested a number of ways to tackle systemic racism. This included developing the tools to understand and recognise how systemic racism and white supremacy operate within each person and in everyday life, changing the way in which white children are taught about racism, having employers and service providers adopt special programmes or special measures within their organisation to combat systemic racism, and ensuring diverse and inclusive organisations.[48]

The health care system in Ottawa, which recognises racism as a public health issue experienced worldwide, has an online programme called *have THAT talk about Racism*, which is available in various languages and includes an activity guide and resources.[49]

In addition to these government-led initiatives, the private sector in Canada is also working towards eradicating systemic racism through, for example, the development of The Micropedia of Microaggressions,[50] which is an online encyclopaedia designed to highlight the pervasiveness and harm of micro-aggressions with tips on how to change behaviours.[51]

The Canadian Centre for Diversity and Inclusion have developed a toolkit to encourage the formation of diversity, equity and inclusion (DE&I) councils in the workplace, which would develop DE&I plans, with training and education programmes for all employees.[52] Law firms have also developed training programmes which go beyond providing traditional harassment training, and are working with companies to ensure that their corporate culture is anti-racist, free from sexual harassment, and a place of safety and respect for all.[53]

Canada's public and private sectors are therefore attempting to address systemic, or institutional, racism through education and training at various levels in society.

---

48 Discussion paper on systemic racism in 2023 13–14.

49 See Ottawa Public Health, *have THAT talk about Racism* https://www.ottawapublichealth.ca/en/public-health-services/have-that-talk-about-racism.aspx#Have-THAT-talk-about-racism-activity-guide (accessed on 29 May 2025).

50 Visit the site on http://themicropedia.org.

51 Toronto Metropolitan University, *The Micropedia of Microaggressions Launches to Shed Light on a Subtle but Commonly Experienced Form of Discrimination*, 7 December 2021 https://www.torontomu.ca/diversity/news-events/2021/12/the-micropedia-of-microaggressions-launches-to-shed-light-on-a-s/ (accessed on 29 May 2025).

52 Canadian Centre for Diversity and Inclusion, *Diversity & inclusion councils: Toolkit for diversity and inclusion practitioners*, September 2017 https://ccdi.ca/media/1072/20170831-ccdi-diversity-council-toolkit-final-v3.pdf (accessed on 29 May 2025).

53 Forte Workplace Law launched StandUP Teams in 2019. See https://standupteams.ca/ and Catherine Skrzypinski, *Canada: HR Should Address Microaggressions in DE&I Training*, 23 February 2023 https://www.shrm.org/topics-tools/news/canada-hr-address-microaggressions-dei-training (accessed on 29 May 2025).

2.5 Conclusions as to the Canadian Legal Framework

In a matter that was heard by the Human Rights Tribunal of Ontario on a racial profiling and discrimination complaint brought against the Toronto Police Service, the Tribunal held that:[54]

> Allegations of discrimination on the basis of race are notoriously difficult to prove because in most cases, discrimination because of race is not overt and manifests in subtle ways. People who honestly believe that they are not prejudiced can nevertheless treat racialized people differently, based on responses which they may not be consciously aware of.
>
> ...
>
> While it is relatively easy to demonstrate the existence of systemic discrimination based on race, in a particular case, it can be much more difficult to determine if the specific encounter was influenced by a person's appearance. In a case under the Code, it is necessary for the applicant to prove the allegation. To do this there must be actual evidence, which in most cases will be circumstantial evidence but which must still be clear and cogent.

What the Tribunal tells us in its decision is that clear and cogent evidence of discrimination is precisely what makes micro-aggressions difficult to prosecute, and why anti-discrimination policies and education are so important when combatting micro-aggressions. Canada recognises that anti-discrimination legislation, and the prosecution of discriminatory practices, is insufficient to eradicate the "subtle scent of discrimination",[55] which seeps into everyday life and stains an entire system and society.

3 New Zealand

3.1 New Zealand's Anti-discrimination Law

The prohibition against discrimination in New Zealand is governed by its Human Rights Act.[56] However, the prosecution of discrimination is explained by New Zealand's Court of Appeal in *Quilter v Attorney-General*[57] as follows:

54 *Fitzgerald v Toronto Police Services Board* 2019 HRTO 22 paras 96 and 98.

55 *Basi v Canadian National Railway Co. (No. 1)* (1988), 9 CHRR D/5029 (CHRT) paras 38493.

56 Act 82 of 1993.

57 [1997] NZCA 207; [1998] 1 NZLR 523.

> Discrimination as such is not defined in the Human Rights Act. Some guidance to its meaning can be found in section 65,[58] which deals with the subject of indirect discrimination. That section speaks of conduct and other things having the 'effect of treating a person or group of persons differently on one of the prohibited grounds of discrimination'. The section does not expressly identify the person or group with whom the necessary comparison is to be made, but that must be either persons generally or another person or group whose treatment is logically relevant to the person or group alleging discrimination.
>
> The essence of discrimination lies in difference of treatment in comparable circumstances. For discrimination to occur one person or group of persons must be treated differently from another person or group of persons. Of course, difference of treatment will not necessarily in itself amount to discrimination; and not all discrimination will be unlawful. In considering whether there is discrimination, it is necessary to define two things: first, the subject matter of and, second, the basis for the alleged discrimination.[59]

New Zealand's Human Rights Act prohibits discrimination on the grounds of sex, marital status, religious belief, ethical belief, colour, race, ethnic or national origins, disability, age, political opinion, employment status, family status, and sexual orientation.[60] The prohibition of discrimination on the aforementioned grounds, however, is limited to employment matters,[61] partnerships,[62] industrial and professional associations, qualifying and vocational training bodies,[63] access to places, vehicles and facilities,[64] the provision of goods and services,[65] the provision of land, housing and other accommodation,[66] and access to educational establishments.[67]

58 Sec 65 (indirect discrimination) of the New Zealand Human Rights Act of 1993: "Where any conduct, practice, requirement, or condition that is not apparently in contravention of any provision of this Part has the effect of treating a person or group of persons differently on 1 of the prohibited grounds of discrimination in a situation where such treatment would be unlawful under any provision of this Part other than this section, that conduct, practice, condition, or requirement shall be unlawful under that provision unless the person whose conduct or practice is in issue, who imposes the condition or requirement, establishes good reason for it".

59 *Quilter v Attorney-General* [1997] NZCA 207; [1998] 1 NZLR 523 573.

60 Sec 21(1) of the New Zealand Human Rights Act.

61 Secs 22 to 35 of the New Zealand Human Rights Act.

62 Sec 36 of the New Zealand Human Rights Act.

63 Secs 37 to 41 of the New Zealand Human Rights Act.

64 Secs 42 and 43 of the New Zealand Human Rights Act.

65 Secs 44 to 52 of the New Zealand Human Rights Act.

66 Secs 53 to 56 of the New Zealand Human Rights Act.

67 Secs 57 to 60 of the New Zealand Human Rights Act.

As with both the Canadian and German anti-discrimination legislation, prohibited discriminatory practices in New Zealand's Human Rights Act are limited to certain places and instances. Furthermore, discrimination hinges on differential treatment in comparable circumstances, which, from a micro-aggression perspective, makes it difficult to prosecute individual slights, which is the form that most often characterises them.

3.2 New Zealand's Legal Treatment of Racial Harassment

Section 63 of the New Zealand Human Rights Act deals with racial harassment and states that:

> (1) It shall be unlawful for any person to use language (whether written or spoken), or visual material, or physical behaviour that –
> - expresses hostility against, or brings into contempt or ridicule, any other person on the ground of the colour, race, or ethnic or national origins of that person; and
> - is hurtful or offensive to that other person (whether or not that is conveyed to the first-mentioned person); and
> - is either repeated, or of such a significant nature, that it has a detrimental effect on that other person in respect of any of the areas to which this subsection is applied by subsection (2).
>
> The areas to which subsection (1) applies are –
> - the making of an application for employment:
> - employment, which term includes unpaid work:
> - participation in, or the making of an application for participation in, a partnership:
> - membership, or the making of an application for membership, of an industrial union or professional or trade association:
> - access to any approval, authorisation, or qualification:
> - vocational training, or the making of an application for vocational training:
> - access to places, vehicles, and facilities:
> - access to goods and services:
> - access to land, housing, or other accommodation:
> - education:
> - participation in fora for the exchange of ideas and information.

Because of the use of the word "and" joining sections 63(1)(a) to (c) of the New Zealand Human Rights Act together, the subsections must be read conjunctively. Therefore, all three of the elements created by these subsections must be present in order to establish racial harassment.[68] According to New Zealand's Human Rights Review Tribunal in *Singh v McKee*,[69] a complainant must be able to establish, on a balance of probabilities that:[70] the defendant used language that either expressed hostility against the complainant or brought the complainant into contempt or ridicule on the ground of race, or ethnic, or national origin;[71] the language was hurtful or offensive to the complainant;[72] and the language was either repeated or of such a significant nature that it had a detrimental effect on the complainant in respect of any of the areas outlined in section 63(2) of the Human Rights Act.

Although a subjective test is used to determine whether or not the impugned language is hurtful or offensive to the complainant, that alone cannot establish racial harassment. Only once all of the elements are established – which includes the application of an objective test to determine an expression of hostility or bringing into contempt or ridicule – does such conduct amount to racial harassment. Racial harassment is also limited to the areas set out in section 63(2) of the Act, and requires that the impugned language either be repeated or serious enough to have a detrimental effect on those areas. This would therefore make the prosecution of micro-aggressions under section 63 difficult given their subtlety.

3.3 The New Zealand Legal Treatment of Racial Disharmony

Section 61 of the Human Rights Act addresses racial disharmony and provides that:

> (1) It shall be unlawful for any person –
> - to publish or distribute written matter which is threatening, abusive, or insulting, or to broadcast by means of radio or television or other electronic communication words which are threatening, abusive, or insulting; or
> - to use in any public place as defined in section 2(1) of the Summary Offences Act 1981, or within the hearing of persons in any such public place, or at any meeting to which the public are invited or have access, words which are threatening, abusive, or insulting; or

68 *Singh v McKee* [2024] NZHRRT 3 para 12.

69 [2024] NZHRRT 3.

70 *Singh v McKee* [2024] NZHRRT 3 para 13.

71 This is an objective enquiry. See *Singh v McKee* [2024] NZHRRT 3 para 36.

72 This is a subjective enquiry. See *Singh v McKee* [2024] NZHRRT 3 para 42.

– to use in any place words which are threatening, abusive, or insulting if the person using the words knew or ought to have known that the words were reasonably likely to be published in a newspaper, magazine, or periodical or broadcast by means of radio or television, –

– being matter or words likely to excite hostility against or bring into contempt any group of persons in or who may be coming to New Zealand on the ground of the colour, race, or ethnic or national origins of that group of persons.

It shall not be a breach of subsection (1) to publish in a newspaper, magazine, or periodical or broadcast by means of radio or television or other electronic communication a report relating to the publication or distribution of matter by any person or the broadcast or use of words by any person, if the report of the matter or words accurately conveys the intention of the person who published or distributed the matter or broadcast or used the words.

The above provision is concerned with the publication or broadcasting of words that are "threatening, abusive, or insulting". Because of the word "or" joining sections 61(1)(a) to (c) together, the subsections may be read disjunctively, meaning that each subsection could amount to racial disharmony separately.

In *Wall v Fairfax New Zealand Ltd*,[73] the High Court held that in order for a publication, in terms of section 61(1)(a), to be unlawful it must be objectively threatening, abusive or insulting.[74] It must also be objectively likely to excite hostility against or bring into contempt any group of persons on account of their ethnicity.[75] In order for the aforesaid to happen the impugned publication must be of a "serious" nature, while also understanding "contempt" to mean a strong emotional response.[76] The Court explained further that the word "likely" means a "real and substantial risk that the stated consequence will happen".[77] Most importantly, for purposes of understanding racial disharmony in the context of micro-aggressions, the Court cites *Saskatchewan Human Rights Commission v Whatcott*,[78] where the Supreme Court of Canada held that:

> Hate speech legislation is not aimed at discouraging repugnant or offensive ideas. It does not, for example, prohibit expression which debates the merits

73 [2018] NZHC 104.

74 *Wall v Fairfax New Zealand Ltd* [2018] NZHC 104 para 51.

75 Ibid.

76 *Wall v Fairfax New Zealand Ltd* [2018] NZHC 104 para 52.

77 *Wall v Fairfax New Zealand Ltd* [2018] NZHC 104 para 61.

78 2013 SCC 11, [2013] 1 SCR 467 para 51.

> of reducing the rights of vulnerable groups in society. It only restricts the use of expression exposing them to hatred as a part of that debate. It does not target the ideas, but their mode of expression in public and the effect that this mode of expression may have.[79]

It follows that the New Zealand High Court does not intend to prosecute hate speech that is merely hurtful, thus excluding the prosecution of micro-aggressions under New Zealand's racial disharmony provision.

3.4 New Zealand's Broader Anti-discrimination Policy Frameworks

New Zealand, like Canada and Germany, does not limit its anti-discrimination framework to legislation. It is currently in the process of developing a national action plan against racism.

A community engagement report for developing a national action plan against racism was released by New Zealand's Human Rights Commission in November 2022.[80] The report identifies five pillars in the development of this national policy. The first pillar is the need to support political control by the Māori people over Māori affairs, which includes the need for constitutional transformation and a revision of immigration policies and processes.[81] The second pillar calls for the support of diversity and inclusion, which means recognising and accepting the cultural, religious, ethnic and racial diversity in New Zealand through intersectoral and cross-sectoral work.[82] The third pillar discusses the need for education for a racism-free New Zealand.[83] The fourth pillar requires the upholding of human rights, especially given the inequality experienced in the healthcare system, housing system, employment, education system, in poverty and in criminal justice indicators.[84] The fifth and last pillar requires that the national policy addresses the transnational nature of racism, with a particular focus on the impact and potential that mainstream

---

79 *Wall v Fairfax New Zealand Ltd* [2018] NZHC 104 para 49.

80 New Zealand Human Rights Commission, *Community Engagement Report for developing a National Action Plan Against Racism*, November 2022 https://tikatangata.org.nz/cms/assets/Documents/Reports-and-Inquiry/Race-and-Ethnicity/Large-Print_Ki-te-whaiao-ke-te-ao-Marama_Summary-Report_PDF.pdf (accessed 31 May 2025).

81 Community Engagement Report for developing a National Action Plan Against Racism 56–59.

82 Community Engagement Report for developing a National Action Plan Against Racism 60–64.

83 Community Engagement Report for developing a National Action Plan Against Racism 65–66.

84 Community Engagement Report for developing a National Action Plan Against Racism 67–73.

and social media have on racism. This includes the way in which ethnic groups and individuals are represented on screen, often being portrayed in negative and stereotypical ways.[85]

In addition to developing a National Action Plan, the New Zealand Council for Educational Research, which falls under the Ministry of Education, created an online self-review toolkit called Wellbeing@School (W@S).[86] The Council aimed to conduct a rapid review survey to see if it could introduce additional constructs to W@S to conceptualise, operationalise, and measure racism in schools.

There are also private organisations that promote diversity and inclusion in workplaces through training, resources, and awards that recognise exemplary practices in diversity management.[87]

3.5 Conclusions as to New Zealand's Legal Framework

New Zealand has a robust anti-discrimination legislative framework, but recognises the need for additional measures in order to truly address systemic and institutionalised racism. Like in most jurisdictions, New Zealand's legislative framework is unable to prosecute micro-aggressions in an effort to balance conflicting rights. It is for that reason that New Zealand, like Germany and Canada, aims to address systemic racism through policy and education.

4 The Netherlands

4.1 The Netherlands' Anti-discrimination Law

The Netherlands' anti-discrimination legislation is the General Equal Treatment Act, which prohibits both direct[88] and indirect[89] discrimination

85 Community Engagement Report for developing a National Action Plan Against Racism 74–76.

86 New Zealand Council for Educational Research, *A rapid review of racism in schools: Working paper*, 2020 https://wellbeingatschool.org.nz/sites/default/files/documents/Racism-in-schools-Rapid-review-working-paper_0.pdf (accessed 29 May 2025).

87 For example Diversity Works NZ. See their website at https://diversityworksnz.org.nz/.

88 Article 1b of the General Equal Treatment Act: "direct discrimination: if a person is treated differently from another person who is, has been or would be treated in a comparable situation, on the grounds of religion, belief, political opinion, race, sex, nationality, hetero- or homosexual orientation or marital status".

89 Article 1c of the General Equal Treatment Act: "indirect discrimination: if an apparently neutral provision, standard or practice particularly affects persons with a particular

that amounts to a differential treatment of people on the grounds of religion, belief, political opinion, race, sex, nationality, hetero- or homosexual orientation or marital status. Given that the Netherlands is a member state of the European Union, it, like Germany, is subject to the same anti-discrimination law requirements set out in the European Commission reports referred to earlier.[90]

The prohibition against discrimination extends to intimidation and sexual intimidation.[91] Discrimination is, however, only prohibited in the filling of a vacancy,[92] employment mediation,[93] employment relationships and promotions,[94] in terms of the Civil Servants Act,[95] in employment and working conditions,[96] in training and education,[97] in access to the liberal profession,[98] in membership of an association of employees, employers and professionals,[99] in access to goods or services[100] and in social protection.[101]

4.2 The Netherlands' Legal Treatment of Intimidation

In terms of article 1A(2) of the General Equal Treatment Act, intimidation means "behaviour that is related to the qualities or behaviour referred to in Article 1, paragraph 1, part b,[102] and that has the purpose or effect of violating the dignity of the person and of creating an intimidating, hostile, insulting, humiliating or offensive environment".

It is important to note that the above form of discrimination is limited to the areas outlined in article 5 of the General Equal Treatment Act. There is very little case law that deals with article 1A(2) of the General Equal Treatment Act, and the cases that do exist concern "bullying" or "undesirable behaviour"

religion, belief, political opinion, race, gender, nationality, hetero- or homosexual orientation or marital status in comparison with other persons".

90 See 1.1 above.

91 Article 1A of the General Equal Treatment Act.

92 Article 5(1)(a) of the General Equal Treatment Act.

93 Article 5(1)(b) of the General Equal Treatment Act.

94 Article 5(1)(c) and 5(1)(g) of the General Equal Treatment Act.

95 Article 5(1)(d) of the General Equal Treatment Act.

96 Articles 5(1)(e) and 5(1)(h) of the General Equal Treatment Act.

97 Articles 5(1)(f) of the General Equal Treatment Act.

98 Article 6 of the General Equal Treatment Act.

99 Article 6a of the General Equal Treatment Act.

100 Article 7 of the General Equal Treatment Act.

101 Article 7A of the General Equal Treatment Act.

102 Article 1(1)(b) of the General Equal Treatment Act refers to "direct distinction" which reads: "if a person is treated in a manner other than a person is or would be treated in a comparable situation, on the basis of the religion, belief, political opinion, race, sex, nationality, heterosexual or homosexual orientation or marital status".

in the workplace, which are prosecuted under intimidation.[103] Intimidation is an overt form of discrimination, whereas micro-aggressions are usually covert.

4.3 The Netherlands' Law on Group Insult and Incitement of Hatred

The incitement of hatred, like in all of the jurisdictions previously mentioned, is criminalised in the Dutch Criminal Code. However, in addition to incitement, the Netherlands also criminalises public insults made against a protected group, which attracts a fine or prison sentence of up to two years.

Articles 137c and 137d of the Dutch Criminal Code read as follows:

> Article 137c
>
> Any person who, in public, either verbally or in writing or through images, deliberately makes insulting statements about a group of people because of their race, their religion or beliefs, their hetero- or homosexual orientation or their physical, psychological or intellectual disability, shall be punished by a prison sentence of up to one year or a fine of the third category.
>
> If the act is committed by a person who makes a profession or habit of it or by two or more persons acting together, a prison sentence of up to two years or a fine of the fourth category shall be imposed.
>
> Article 137d
>
> He who publicly, verbally or in writing or by image, incites hatred or discrimination against people or violent action against the person or property of people on the grounds of their race, religion or belief, gender, hetero- or homosexual orientation or physical, psychological or intellectual disability, shall be punished by a prison sentence of not more than two years or a fine of the fourth category.
>
> If the act is committed by a person who makes a profession or habit of it or by two or more persons acting together, a prison sentence of up to four years or a fine of the fourth category shall be imposed.

The wording on the prohibition of incitement to hatred is not dissimilar to that of Germany's, which is not surprising as they are both EU member states, but also not too dissimilar to that of Canada.

In order for an act to amount to an offence in terms of article 137c, an insulting statement must be made deliberately against a group of people in public. According to the Dutch Supreme Court,[104] a statement is considered insulting

103 ECLI:NL:RBDHA:2022:2537 and ECLI:NL:GHDHA:2023:2911.

104 ECLI:NL:HR:2021:1036 Supreme Court, 06-07-2021, 20/03005.

to a group of people if it is "unnecessarily offensive" and attacks the self-esteem of or discredits a group for the sole reason that the group is of a particular race or religion, or has a particular belief, hetero- or homosexual orientation, physical, psychological or intellectual disability.[105] Additionally, the Supreme Court held that an accused person must have intended to insult the group, and that the insult must have been "in public".[106] "In public" is understood by Dutch courts to mean to "bring to the attention of the public".[107] In other words, if an insulting statement was made during a closed event where the statement then subsequently broadcast on radio or television, the court is required to consider the circumstances of the case and determine whether the insulting statement was intended to be brought "to the attention of the public" by the accused. The culmination of those elements is what produces a guilty verdict.

When considering whether or not micro-aggressions are prosecutable under the above offence, it is important to note that the group element, along with the requirements that the statement/s be made publicly with the intention to be unnecessarily offensive, may make it difficult for micro-insults and micro-invalidations to fit the definition.

4.4 The Netherlands' Broader Anti-discrimination Policy Frameworks

As part of the Netherland's broader anti-discrimination framework, the Kingdom has a National Action Plan on Human Rights,[108] with non-discrimination and equal treatment[109] addressed as part of the policy. The Netherlands still struggles with institutionalised racism which rears its head in racialised traditions such as *Zwarte Piet*,[110] Santa's black helper, and, perhaps more prominently in government institutions such as in border control where racial profiling is still an issue.[111]

105 Ibid paras 8.4.2–8.4.3.

106 Ibid para 8.4.5.1.

107 Ibid para 8.4.5.2.

108 Dutch Ministry of the Interior and Kingdom Relations, *National Action Plan on Human Rights*, February 2014 https://www.humanrights.dk/sites/humanrights.dk/files/media/document/Netherlands%20NHRAP%202014%20English.pdf (accessed on 29 May 2025).

109 National Action Plan on Human Rights 31.

110 Van Gelder (2020) https://universonline.nl/nieuws/2020/06/16/institutional-racism-dutch-problem/ (accessed on 29 May 2025).

111 Journalists for Justice (2023) https://jfjustice.net/dutch-border-controls-illegally-discriminate-against-black-people-court-rules/ (accessed on 29 May 2025).

According to the Netherlands Institute for Human Rights,[112] programmes used in educational institutions and training,[113] as well as workplace training programmes for the private[114] and public sectors,[115] and equal treatment in the use of algorithm programmes,[116] are some of the ways in which the Netherlands aims to reduce institutionalised racism, and with it, micro-aggressions.

4.5 Conclusions as to the Netherlands' Legal Framework

The Netherlands appears to have more of an issue with covert,[117] as opposed to overt, racism which would include micro-aggressions. However, the country's legal framework, like with every other jurisdiction that has been analysed thus far, only allows for the prosecution of overt discrimination. Institutionalised and systemic racism are addressed in the Netherlands' broader anti-discrimination framework, which focuses on educating people, and re-programming systems, against racial biases.

5 Namibia

5.1 Namibia's Anti-discrimination Law

Namibia, with a similar history of racial injustice and discrimination to that of South Africa, has the Racial Discrimination Prohibition Act[118] as its primary anti-discrimination legislation. In this short Act comprising of only 23 sections, Namibia, like all of the jurisdictions analysed here, prohibits certain discriminatory practices set out in sections 2 to 9 of its Act against a "racial group"

---

112 College voor de Rechten van de Mens, *Jaarverslag 2023*, April 2024 https://publicaties.mensenrechten.nl/publicatie/138c98d0-137d-4b3d-a718-b724bcedb16b (accessed 29 May 2025).

113 *De Toolbox Mensenrechten op School (voor primair en voortgezet onderwijs) en de Toolbox Mensenrechten in het mbo* (Toolbox Human Rights in School (for primary and secondary education) and the Toolbox Human Rights in Vocational Education and Training). See *Jaarverslag* 2023 21.

114 *Selecteren zonder Vooroordelen* (Select Without Prejudice programme). See *Jaarverslag* 2023 21.

115 *Programma Vooroordelen Voorbij* (Beyond Prejudice programme). See *Jaarverslag* 2023 21.

116 *Programma Digitalisering & Mensenrechten* (Digitalisation & Human Rights programme). See *Jaarverslag* 2023 28.

117 Van Gelder (2020) https://universonline.nl/nieuws/2020/06/16/institutional-racism-dutch-problem/ (accessed on 29 May 2025).

118 Act 26 of 1991.

defined as "a group of persons defined by reference to colour, race, nationality or ethnic or national origin".[119] Prohibited practices, in terms of the Racial Discrimination Prohibition Act, include discrimination in respect of access to and use of public amenities and facilities,[120] in the provision of goods and services,[121] in the sale or leasing of immoveable property,[122] in access to educational institutions,[123] in access to medical institutions,[124] in employment,[125] in access to associations,[126] and in access to religious services.[127]

5.2 Namibian Legal Treatment of Racial Disharmony

Namibia, like New Zealand, has a prohibition against racial disharmony, which is in effect a hate speech clause. The prohibition against the incitement of racial disharmony is covered by section 11 of the Racial Discrimination Prohibition Act, which provides as follows:

> No person shall publicly use any language or publish or distribute any written matter or display any article or do any act or thing with the intent to –
> - threaten or insult any person or group of persons on the ground that such person belongs or such persons belong to a particular racial group; or
> - cause, encourage or incite hatred between different racial groups or persons belonging to different racial groups; or
> - disseminate ideas based on racial superiority.
>
> For the purposes of subsection (1) "article" shall include any flag, insignia or emblem.
>
> No person shall establish, support or be a member of or participate in the activities of an organisation or movement of which the aim is to disseminate any ideas based on racial superiority aimed at members of any particular racial group or engage in activities aimed at causing, bringing about, promoting or contributing to any such disseminating of such ideas or engaging in such activities.

119 Sec 1 of the Racial Discrimination Prohibition Act.
120 Sec 2 of the Racial Discrimination Prohibition Act.
121 Sec 3 of the Racial Discrimination Prohibition Act.
122 Sec 4 of the Racial Discrimination Prohibition Act.
123 Sec 5 of the Racial Discrimination Prohibition Act.
124 Sec 6 of the Racial Discrimination Prohibition Act.
125 Sec 7 of the Racial Discrimination Prohibition Act.
126 Sec 8 of the Racial Discrimination Prohibition Act.
127 Sec 9 of the Racial Discrimination Prohibition Act.

For purposes of this discussion on micro-aggressions, it is interesting to note that the original wording of section 11 of the Racial Discrimination Prohibition Act was amended in 1998[128] due to a declaration of unconstitutionality by the Namibian High Court in *S v Smith*.[129] The Namibian High Court, like the South African Constitutional Court in *Qwelane*,[130] found section 11 to be overbroad, thereby infringing upon the right to freedom of expression.[131] The Namibian High Court proceeded to remove the following words from the original section 11: "ridicule", "disharmony or feelings of hostility", and "ill-will".[132] This is a clear indication of the Namibian legal system's unwillingness to prosecute micro-aggressions, which are more likely to fit the category of the deleted words.

5.3 Namibian Broader Anti-discrimination Policy Frameworks

As part of its broader fight against discrimination, the Namibian government implemented a National Human Rights Action Plan from 2015 to 2019.[133] Some of the Action Plan's key interventions included undertaking public education and awareness campaigns aimed at eradicating discriminatory practices and incorporating human rights and tolerance education into school curricula.[134]

5.4 Conclusions as to Namibia's Legal Framework

Because of Namibia's history, its anti-discrimination framework aims to address prejudice (and racial prejudice in particular) to the furthest extent possible. Shortcomings in its legislative framework were recognised in the country's National Human Rights Action Plan, which aimed to review the

---

128 Sec 1 of Racial Discrimination Prohibition Amendment Act 26 of 1998.

129 *S v Smith and Others* 1996 NR 367 (HC).

130 *Qwelane v South African Human Rights Commission and Another* (CCT 13/20) [2021] ZACC 22; 2021 6 SA 579 (CC); 2022 2 BCLR 129 (CC).

131 *S v Smith and Others* 1996 NR 367 (HC) 373C–E.

132 The original wording of sec 11, in Act 26 of 1991, read as follows: "No person shall publicly use any language or publish or distribute any written matter or display any article or do any act or thing with intent to – a. threaten, ridicule or insult any person or group of persons on the ground that such person belongs or such group of persons belong to a particular racial group; or b. cause, encourage or incite disharmony or feelings of hostility, hatred or ill-will between different racial groups or persons belonging to different racial groups; c. disseminate ideas based on racial superiority".

133 National Human Rights Action Plan: Republic of Namibia: 2015–2019 https://ombudsman.org.na/wp-content/uploads/2022/09/NHRAP.pdf (accessed on 29 May 2025).

134 National Human Rights Action Plan 40.

Racial Discrimination Prohibition Act and enact new legislation against discrimination.[135] The key interventions listed in the Action Plan also aim to address societal attitudes by educating the population. However, like every other jurisdiction discussed here, Namibia does not provide for the prosecution of micro-aggressions, but rather chooses to address them through education in its National Action Plan.

6 Summary of Comparative Analysis

It is a delicate balancing act to level out the right to equality, dignity and freedom from discrimination, with the right to freedom of expression. In every one of the five jurisdictions discussed above either legislation or the courts have been clear about the fact that prosecuting "hurtful" language or language that "ridicules" or causes "disharmony or feelings of hostility" or that came from a place of "ill-will" would be an infringement on the right to freedom of expression. This would make it nearly impossible to prosecute (in criminal courts) or litigate (in civil courts) micro-aggressions.

However, in an attempt to address and eventually eradicate such underhanded and prevalent discrimination, each of the jurisdictions has a broader anti-discrimination policy framework. This includes national action plans against discrimination. Generally speaking, each of these broader frameworks attempts to address institutionalised and systemic racism, which would include micro-aggressions, through the employment of public education campaigns, data collection, specialised school curricula, workplace diversity monitoring mechanisms and labour laws with complaints mechanisms, training for the private and public sectors, legislative and policy reform, and complaints and accountability mechanisms, including civil redress and criminal sanction.

135 National Human Rights Action Plan 41.

CHAPTER 6

The South African Approach to Discrimination, Hate Speech and Harassment

In this chapter, we focus in more depth on the post-apartheid South African Parliament's approach. Apartheid was characterised by daily indignities suffered by the majority black population, over and above being disenfranchised, marginalised and victimised by the apartheid state apparatus. The South African Constitution can be read as a "never again" proclamation against ever repeating the injustices of apartheid. The Equality Act, its drafting expressly mandated in section 9(4) of the Constitution, aims to concretise this "never again" sentiment. We argue that the Equality Act should be read as an injunction against large-scale, systemic denial of dignity, as well as daily indignities.

1 The Causes of Action Recognised in the South African Equality Act Read against the Aims of This Act

The causes of action recognised in the Equality Act should be read against the ostensible purpose of this Act. Anti-discrimination legislation could have a number of purposes including

a) illustrating a symbolic commitment to addressing discrimination;
b) setting up (inexpensive and accessible) complaint resolution mechanisms where (individual, insular, discrete) discrimination complaints may be resolved;
c) facilitating large-scale socio-economic transformation; and
d) facilitating broad and thoroughgoing changes in the hearts and minds of the target population.[1]

---

1 Compare Brand (2000) Autumn *Word and Action* 13; Moseneke (2002) 18 *South African Journal on Human Rights* 309 319 ("[T]he overarching constitutional enterprise of transforming our society into a democratic, non-racial, non-discriminating, egalitarian, socially just and *caring* society (our emphasis); Hocking (1995) 15 *Proctor* 19 21 (who identifies the barriers to a truly non-discriminatory society as "personal attitudes, subtle perceptions and entrenched male focused value systems"); Dror (1958) 33 *Tulane Law Review* 787 788 (who states that "social change" refers to changes in social structure or *culture*); and Klare (1998) 14 *South African Journal on Human Rights* 146 at 150 (he talks of a multicultural, *caring* society). See Kok 2008, where these themes are unpacked in much more detail.

 | HTTPS://DOI.ORG/10.1163/9789004757523-007

In the context of this book, the fourth purpose is particularly relevant.[2]

It is clear from an analysis of a number of provisions in the Equality Act that the legislature also aimed to bring about changes in the "hearts and minds" of South Africans with the enactment of this Act. The Preamble explicitly expresses the wish that the Act will remove the "pain and suffering" brought "to the great majority of our people", as well as the "systemic inequalities and unfair discrimination" that "remain deeply embedded in social structures, practices and *attitudes*",[3] and that the Act will restore people's lost dignity. The Preamble explicitly notes that "this Act endeavours to facilitate the transition to a democratic society, united in its diversity, *marked by human relations that are caring and compassionate*".[4] A number of the examples listed in sections 7 and 8 at least implicitly address attitudinal discrimination.[5] The sections in the Act dealing with the promotion of equality also, at least implicitly, engage anticipated attitudinal changes.[6]

It should also be emphasised that the Act has as one of its goals the establishment of forums where discrimination disputes may be raised and resolved. A number of provisions in section 2 of the Act (which contains the objects of

---

2 This kind of transformation would for example include issues such as the eradication of "unjust joking" as referred to by Verwoerd & Verwoerd (1994) 23 *Agenda* 67. The (then) Deputy Minister of Justice and Constitutional Development seemed to have both "types" of discrimination in mind when she spoke during the consideration of the Bill in the National Council of Provinces, 28 January 2000 (reproduced in Gutto (2001) 71 and further.) The Deputy Minister said that the "express goal with this legislation is the creation of a society based on respect for the dignity and equal worth of all human beings. The underlying tenet of the Bill is the belief ... that we can eliminate systemic forms of unfair discrimination inherited from a past fraught with prejudice and bigotry and ... that we can prevent and prohibit any new forms of disadvantage that may arise". Also compare the "Memorandum on the Objects of the Promotion of Equality and Prevention of Unfair Discrimination Bill" that accompanied Bill B57B-99 (ISBN 0 621 29135 8): "This Bill is drafted to give effect to the letter and spirit of the Constitution, especially the founding values of *achieving* equality and *human dignity*" (our emphasis). The Supreme Court of Appeal offers a similar (oblique) interpretation of the aim of the Act in *Minister of Environmental Affairs and Tourism v George* 2007 (3) SA 62 (SCA) para 3: "The statute's objects are to give effect to the letter and spirit of the Constitution's equality promise ..."

3 Our emphasis.

4 Our emphasis.

5 Consider secs 7(a) ("the dissemination of any propaganda or idea, which propounds the *racial superiority or inferiority of any person*, including incitement to, or participation in, any form of racial violence"); 8(a) ("gender-based violence"); 8(b) ("female genital mutilation"); and 8(d) ("any practice, including traditional, customary or religious practice, *which impairs the dignity of women* and undermines equality between women and men, including the *undermining of the dignity* and well-being of the girl child" (our emphasis)).

6 Secs 2(b)(ii); 2(e); 3(1)(a); and 24–28.

the Act) may be read to create this aim. Section 2(b)(i) states that the Act aims at giving effect to the letter and spirit of the Constitution, in particular "the equal enjoyment of all rights and freedoms *by every person*".[7] This subsection anticipates a procedure whereby individual claimants will be able to ensure the enjoyment of their human rights. Section 2(b)(iv) contains another object of the Act: "the prevention of unfair discrimination and protection of human dignity as contemplated in sections 9 and 10 of the Constitution". This subsection, read with sections 2(d),[8] 2(f),[9] 4(1)(b),[10] 16 and the regulations to the Act,[11] makes it clear that the Act aims at the creation of inexpensive, accessible, informal dispute resolution mechanisms (equality courts).

If the sections of the Equality Act that aim at changing hearts and minds and that create inexpensive, accessible and informal dispute resolution mechanisms are read together, it means that equality courts should serve as open forums where micro-aggressions are adjudicated and pronounced upon, and remedies awarded to address the micro-aggressions effectively. The Equality Act lists wide-ranging remedies, over and above the general injunction that any "appropriate order" may be made.[12] These remedies could include an apology, an order that the offender must attend and complete a diversity and inclusion education course, the payment of damages to the complainant or to a body that advocates for inclusion and diversity.

The Equality Act establishes the civil causes of action of unfair discrimination, hate speech and harassment.

(a) Discrimination

Discrimination is defined as "any act or omission, including a policy, law, rule, practice, condition or situation which directly or indirectly (a) imposes burdens, obligations or disadvantage on; or (b) withholds benefits, opportunities or advantages from, any person on one or more of the prohibited grounds".

The Act contains an extensive and open-ended list of prohibited grounds: "(a) race, gender, sex, pregnancy, marital status, ethnic or social origin, colour, sexual orientation, age, disability, religion, conscience, belief, culture, language

7 Our emphasis.

8 "[T]o provide for procedures for the determination of circumstances under which discrimination is unfair".

9 "[T]o provide remedies for victims of unfair discrimination, hate speech and harassment and persons whose right to equality has been infringed".

10 "In the adjudication of any proceedings which are instituted in terms of or under this Act, the following principles should apply: (*b*) access to justice to all persons in relevant judicial and other dispute resolution forums".

11 GN No R764, *Government Gazette* No 25065, 2003-06-13.

12 Sec 21(2) of the Equality Act.

and birth; or (b) any other ground where discrimination based on that other ground – (i) causes or perpetuates systemic disadvantage; (ii) undermines human dignity; or (iii) adversely affects the equal enjoyment of a person's rights and freedoms in a serious manner that is comparable to discrimination on a ground in paragraph (a)".

Read literally, and if "burden" is read as including psychological harm, everyday insults that are based on one or more of these prohibited grounds meet the definition of discrimination in the Equality Act. To illustrate practically the kind of incidents we have in mind, take as an example a school playground taunt of "fatty fatty" expressed towards an overweight learner. Arguably, a psychological burden is imposed on a person based on the (unlisted) prohibited ground of weight or physical appearance.[13] So, "discrimination" seems to be established. The next step is then to work out if the discrimination is unfair. The Equality Act contains a long list of factors to be considered in working out the fairness or unfairness of the impugned discrimination. These are set out in section 14 of the Act.

According to the Equality Act, once a complainant makes out a *prima facie* case of discrimination, the respondent must either prove that the discrimination did not take place, or that the discrimination was fair.[14] Section 14 of the Act contains a number of factors to be considered to determine the fairness or unfairness of the alleged discrimination. The prohibition of discrimination is not qualified in the Equality Act. The Act states emphatically that the Act applies to all cases of private and public discrimination.[15]

Should a complainant approach the equality court based on this taunt and argue that discrimination occurred, the court would have to consider the fairness or unfairness of the taunt. The more appropriate causes of action to consider in this regard would be hate speech and harassment. The causes of action of hate speech and harassment do not contain the qualifier "unfair", but other qualifiers hem in the otherwise broad application.

(b) Hate speech

Hate speech is prohibited in these terms: "no person may publish, propagate, advocate or communicate words based on one or more of the prohibited

---

13 See Pieterse (2000) 16 *South African Journal on Human Rights* 121 on the recognition of physical appearance as a prohibited ground of discrimination.

14 Sec 13. The determination of fairness or unfairness as described in the Equality Act seemingly does not apply to hate speech (sec 15), but see the discussion of *Qwelane* below, where it seems that the South African Constitutional Court incorporated a contextual enquiry into the determination of hate speech. This contextual enquiry comes very close to a "fairness/unfairness" enquiry.

15 Secs 26 and 27.

grounds, against any person, that could reasonably be construed to demonstrate a clear intention to be harmful or to incite harm and promote or propagate hatred".

(c) Harassment

Harassment is defined as "unwanted conduct which is persistent or serious and demeans, humiliates or creates a hostile or intimidating environment or is calculated to induce submission by actual or threatened adverse consequences and which is related to (a) sex, gender or sexual orientation, or (b) a person's membership or presumed membership of a group identified by one or more of the prohibited grounds or a characteristic associated with such group".

The "fatty fatty" taunt could arguably meet the definition of all three of these causes of action, if a court does not take an unduly strained approach to the kind of conduct that the legislature had in mind when it enacted the Equality Act. However, should an equality court be open to an argument that the claim be dismissed based on the maxim *de minimis non curat lex*? The argument could be based on the lines that life is sometimes hard; that we should all accept that some days will be better than others; that some hardships build character; that these kinds of insults will come our way from time to time; that we should take it on the chin, grin and bear it, and move on. Should a court take cognisance of these implicit considerations contained within *de minimis* when applying the qualifiers to the three causes of action of discrimination, hate speech and harassment?

2 The Interpretation and Application of the Qualifiers (Internal Limitations) to the Causes of Action Recognised in the South African Equality Act

The three causes of action created in the Equality Act all contain a number of qualifiers in their definitions that may be read as a signal by Parliament to filter out at least some complaints. The Equality Act prohibits "unfair" discrimination, "persistent or serious" harassment, and used to prohibit "hurtful" words before its judicial deletion in *Qwelane*.[16]

In this section, we argue that a pro-transformation and pro-diversity interpretation should be given to the qualifiers for discrimination, hate speech and harassment. We also explain how these qualifiers should relate to the maxim *de minimis non curat lex*.

16 But see *Qwelane* where the Constitutional Court has unfortunately excised "hurtful" from the definition of hate speech.

2.1 "Based on a Prohibited Ground"

A qualifier that is important for all three causes of action discussed in this section is "based on a prohibited ground". This qualifier is the reason why "ordinary" insults are not heard in the equality court. One of the purposes of anti-discrimination laws is to combat stereotypes.[17] Most, if not all, stereotypes are found in the prohibited grounds listed and recognised in the Equality Act. The equality courts, as co-facilitators of social transformation, should therefore pay particular care to which prohibited grounds are implicated in the complaints lodged at these courts, and which remedies would be most appropriate to combat the marginalisation, stigmatisation and "othering" exhibited in these complaints.

2.2 "Unfair" Discrimination

The reason for the promulgation of the Equality Act was to give effect to section 9 of the Constitution.[18] The preamble of the Equality Act states that the eradication of social and economic inequalities which were generated in our history by colonialism, apartheid and patriarchy is required. It is also clear from the short title of the Equality Act what its objectives are – the promotion of equality and the prevention of discrimination. The Equality Act also affords reactive measures where people are discriminated against or where the right to equality is breached.[19]

Another objective of the Equality Act is compliance with international law obligations,[20] including, amongst others, the Convention on the Elimination of All Forms of Racial Discrimination and the Convention on the Elimination of All Forms of Discrimination Against Women. In the former, it is stated that there is no justification for racial discrimination, in theory or in practice, anywhere and that all necessary measures should be taken to speedily eliminate racial discrimination in all its forms and manifestations. It also states that each party to the convention undertakes not to defend racial discrimination by any person, but to discourage anything which tends to strengthen racial division. In the Convention on the Elimination of All Forms of Discrimination Against Women, it is stated that each party to the Convention undertakes to condemn

17 See eg Ross-Amato (2002–2003) 29 *William Mitchell Law Review* 569.

18 Sec 2.

19 Kruger (2011) 7 *The Equal Rights Review* 27.

20 Sec 2(h).

discrimination in all its forms and agree to pursue by all appropriate means and without delay a policy of eliminating discrimination against women.

Taking these objectives of the Constitution, the Equality Act and the relevant conventions into consideration, one can hardly disagree with the notion that matters affecting the dignity of a person, such as discrimination on the basis of sex or race, should not be treated lightly.[21] Judicial consideration of so-called trivial violations of constitutional rights can illuminate important principles, and these so-called trivial violations can nurture larger societal problems if left unremedied.[22] Regardless how small the individual wrongs, the collective influence of injuries can be significant and the application of the maxim may result in more violations.[23] Some commentators, therefore, commend the precept *de minimis curet lex*, namely that the law should concern itself with some affronts that appear to be insignificant,[24] since the toleration of even insignificant violations of constitutional rights will have a deteriorating effect on our sense of fundamental rights.[25]

Section 14 contains a basket of factors that need to be considered together to determine whether the respondent has proven fairness. It is firstly stated that taking measures to protect or advance persons previously disadvantaged by unfair discrimination does not constitute unfair discrimination.[26] Section 14(2) then lists different factors that need to be taken into account, namely context,[27] and whether the discrimination reasonably and justifiably differentiates between persons according to objectively determinable criteria, intrinsic to the activity concerned.[28] Other considerations are whether the discrimination impairs human dignity,[29] the impact of the discrimination on the

21 Samuels (1985) *Statute Law Review* 167 168.

22 Bernstein (2010) 62 *Florida Law Review* 895.

23 Inest (2006) 21 *Berkeley Technology Law Journal* 945 955.

24 Bernstein (2010) 62 *Florida Law Review* 895.

25 Guthrie (1898) 41.

26 Sec 14(1) of the South African Equality Act; sec 9(2) of the South African Constitution.

27 Sec 14(2)(a). This includes the social, economic and political circumstances in South Africa. De Vos (2000) 63 *Journal of Contemporary Roman-Dutch Law* 67; De Vos (2000) 117 *South African Law Journal* 17 19.

28 Sec 14(2)(c). This subsection is an attempt to address the concerns of the insurance industry and to distinguish between discrimination and economic differentiation. Some writers opine that this subsection is unconstitutional on the basis that it subtracts from the protection offered by the Constitution. Liebenberg & O'Sullivan (2001) *Acta Juridica* 70 98. See also Kok (2008) 324.

29 Sec 14(3)(a).

complainant,[30] the position of the complainant in society and whether he or she suffers from patterns of disadvantage.[31]

Courts must also take into account the nature and extent of the discrimination,[32] whether the discrimination is systemic in nature,[33] whether the discrimination has a legitimate purpose,[34] whether and to what extent the discrimination achieves its purpose,[35] whether there are less restrictive means to achieve the purpose[36] and whether the respondent has taken reasonable steps to address the disadvantage or accommodate diversity.[37] (At the risk of digressing, it is clear from Constitutional Court caselaw that there is still much uncertainty and divergence regarding the application of the fairness/ unfairness test relating to discrimination.[38] It is also not clear whether newly recognised, unlisted grounds of discrimination are somehow less serious than the explicitly recognised, listed grounds. Socio-economic discrimination is, for example, not listed in the Equality Act, but if one considers the aim of addressing the plight of the country's poor and unemployed, this ground should be regarded as one of the most significant prohibited bases of discrimination.[39])

We have not been able to locate any South African cases relating to unfair discrimination that could plausibly have been met by the *de minimis* defence – in other words, to non-suit a plaintiff based on the trivial nature of the unfair discrimination.[40] Logically, a finding of trivial unfair discrimination cannot follow – a South African court will label insignificant, trivial discrimination as

30 Sec 14(3)(b).

31 Sec 14(3)(c). It is assumed that the only group of people who does not qualify for preferential treatment is able bodied heterosexual white men. Jagwanth (2003) 36 *Connecticut Law Review* 738.

32 Sec 14(3)(d).

33 Sec 14(3)(e).

34 Sec 14(3)(f).

35 Sec 14(3)(g).

36 Sec 14(3)(h). See also the South African Constitution sec 36(1)(e).

37 Sec 14(3)(i).

38 In *S v Jordan* 2002 6 SA 642 (CC) only six of the eleven presiding judges held that the gender discrimination was fair. In *Harksen v Lane* 1998 1 SA 300 (CC) only five of the nine presiding judges held that the discrimination based on marital status was fair.

39 Fredman (2005) 21 *South African Journal on Human Rights* 163.

40 *MEC for Education: Kwazulu-Natal and Others v Pillay* 2007 2 SA 106 (CC) comes the closest to a *de minimis* matter. A 14-year-old high school learner, following a South Indian cultural tradition, had a small nose stud inserted as part of a coming-of-age ceremony. The school objected and required the student's mother to provide written justification. When her explanation was rejected, the student faced the prospect of a disciplinary hearing. *De minimis* is raised by another name in the part of the judgment headed "the severity of the infringement" (para 85 and further). The Court rightly makes short shrift of this defence.

"fair" and dismiss the claim. Where courts should be careful is to properly and sensitively apply the factors set out in section 14 of the Equality Act to determine "fairness" or "unfairness". Constitutional Court judge Yacoob's statement in *Le Roux v Dey* is to the point: "The violation of human dignity in the context of unfair discrimination on any of the grounds listed in the Constitution would be unarguably egregious".[41] A court should be careful to avoid using the factors "whether the discrimination impairs or is likely to impair human dignity";[42] "the impact or likely impact of the discrimination on the complainant";[43] and "the nature and extent of the discrimination",[44] to non-suit a plaintiff. The less serious nature of some kinds of discrimination should rather be reflected in a less-invasive remedy than in non-suiting a plaintiff on a finding of "fair" discrimination or non-suiting a plaintiff based on *de minimis*.

2.3 "Persistent" or "Serious" Harassment

We have not been able to locate any equality court cases that relate to harassment as defined in the Equality Act ("unwanted conduct which is persistent or serious and demeans, humiliates or creates a hostile or intimidating environment or is calculated to induce submission by actual or threatened adverse consequences and which is related to (a) sex, gender or sexual orientation, or (b) a person's membership or presumed membership of a group identified by one or more of the prohibited grounds or a characteristic associated with such group").

In the context of a discussion of the *de minimis* defence, the qualifier "serious" warrants attention. South African labour discrimination laws allow for a single incident to constitute (sexual) harassment if the incident was serious.[45] The Labour Appeal Court decision in *Campbell Scientific Africa (Pty) Ltd v Simmers* is particularly instructive on how the qualifier "serious" should

41 Para 46.

42 Sec 14(3)(a).

43 Sec 14(3)(b).

44 Sec 14(3)(d). It seems as though this section refers to the extent to which the discrimination impairs the complainant's dignity, or the extent of the impact of the discrimination. It possibly also refers to the isolatedness of the incident or the number of persons impacted by the discriminating behaviour.

45 See eg *Campbell Scientific Africa (Pty) Ltd v Simmers* [2016] 1 BLLR 1 (LAC) para 13. In similar fashion, Lukes & Bangs (2014) 24 *Research in Higher Education Journal* 3 argues for the following criteria to recognise a claim for harassment (as a form of a micro-aggression): A faculty member must prove that the micro-aggression was intended towards a marginalised and protected group; a reasonable person would find the micro-aggression harassing; and *the micro-aggression was pervasive or severe* (our emphasis).

be understood. S, L and M were staying at a lodge a considerable distance from their usual workplace. They were contracted to undertake a site survey. On S's account of the events, he asked M once, on their last night at the lodge while they were both outside waiting for L to settle the bill, if she needed a lover for the night. The Labour Appeal Court held that this conduct amounted to sexual harassment and that S's dismissal from his employment was warranted. The Court argued that South Africa's democracy was founded on dignity and the achievement of equality in a non-sexist society.[46] The 1996 Constitution is a transformative document that contains the hope of reimagining power relations to achieve substantive equality.[47] S's advances to M was underlaid by a power differential that favoured S due to his age and gender – M was almost 25 years S's junior.[48] M's dignity was impaired by the insecurity caused by S's conduct – she was nervous given the proximity of the sleeping arrangements at the lodge and she programmed L's number into her phone in case anything should happen that night.[49] A colleague was quite critical of this judgment and thought that S "merely tried his luck" – *de minimis non curat lex* by another name. But this is precisely why the judgment is important and correct – that new standards of behaviour are required if the Constitution's promise of a truly equal society is to be taken seriously.

A case note by Botes,[50] who is rather critical of the Labour Appeal Court's finding in this matter, read with the *Simmers* judgment, leads to the following list of factors to determine if a single incident is serious enough to warrant a finding of (sexual) harassment: (a) if the incident constituted an impairment of the complainant's dignity, (b) the complainant's circumstances; (c) the respective positions of the parties (power differential) in the workplace or other context where the incident took place; (d) if the incident consisted of physical conduct; (e) if the incident constituted *quid pro quo* harassment; (f) the duration of the incident; (g) the risk of any future hostile environment; (h) the subjective reaction of the complainant; (i) was an offensive and humiliating environment created by objectively considering the conduct complained of and all surrounding circumstances; and (j) making a value judgment to ensure fairness to all parties.

46 Para 18.

47 Para 18.

48 Para 27.

49 Para 27.

50 Botes (2017) *Tydskrif vir die Suid-Afrikaanse Reg* 761.

2.4 "Hurtful" Hate Speech

Micro-aggressions would, in most instances, occur as hurtful speech.[51] This section, therefore, warrants a longer discussion, particularly in light of the regrettable decision by the South African Constitutional Court in *Qwelane*.

This section proceeds as follows. The common law of insult is first described. After *Qwelane*, somewhat ironically, pre-1994 apartheid common law now presents more possibilities to address micro-aggressions than post-1994 democratically enacted legislation. After the discussion of the common law of insult, the main holdings from the *Qwelane* judgment are described and then criticised. A part of the criticism relates to a comparison between the common law of insult and the prohibition of hate speech in section 10 of the Equality Act. We conclude by advocating for a legislative response to *Qwelane* to undo its damage to the South African societal transformation project.

(a) The common law of insult

The South African common law on insult is clear and was left untouched by the Constitutional Court in *Le Roux v Dey*. A claimant in a common law case for the intentional impairment of dignity must prove a subjective and an objective element. Subjectively, the complainant must, in fact, have felt insulted. Objectively, a reasonable person must also have felt insulted by the same conduct.[52] The reason given for the objective test is to avoid courts being inundated by trivial actions by hypersensitive complainants;[53] *de minimis*, in other words.

In *Le Roux v Dey*, the Constitutional Court had to consider whether a schoolboy prank complained of by the plaintiff, the deputy principal, was actionable. It was a common law claim based on defamation and insult, not a claim brought in terms of the Equality Act, but similar principles were at play. *De minimis* was implicitly at play in this judgment, as the court had to decide if the prank was of sufficient gravity to warrant the court's sanction. The Court had to reflect on the boundaries between an acceptable and unacceptable joke. The majority judgment made the following distinction (paras 114, 119; emphasis added):

> The real question is whether the reasonable observer will – perhaps while laughing – understand the joke as belittling the plaintiff; as making the plaintiff

---

51 Most of the examples in the table in chapter 2 above relate to hurtful statements.

52 *Le Roux v Dey* 2011 3 SA 274 (CC) para 143. Also see Neethling (2005) 38 *Comparative and International Law Journal of Southern Africa* 220 230.

53 *Le Roux v Dey* para 179.

> look foolish and unworthy of respect; or as exposing the plaintiff to ridicule and contempt ... In principle [*the line*] *is crossed when the joke becomes hurtful* ... In the end it comes down to a value judgment.

The same qualifier appears here as in the pre-*Qwelane* Equality Act – "hurtful" – and there was no issue in this Constitutional Court judgment that this cause of action – the intentional infliction of hurt – was constitutional. (Two of the ten judges parted ways with the majority judgment and would have held that the joke complained of would not have hurt a fictional reasonable deputy principal,[54] and that while children must face the consequences of their actions, it must be done in a manner commensurate with the offence.[55])

The implication of the majority judgment in *Le Roux v Dey* is clear – where words (or conduct) are (subjectively and objectively) hurtful, *de minimis* does not come into play, at least for the common law *actio iniuriarum* for an intentional insult.

South African caselaw presents an inconsistent picture when considering how courts have dealt with the protection of dignity in this context. On the one hand there is the 1958 decision of *R v Walton*,[56] that "in the ordinary hurly-burly of everyday life a man (sic) must be expected to endure minor or trivial insults to his dignity" and the 1989 decision of *De Lange v Costa*,[57] and the 2012 decision of *Masiu v Dos Ramos*,[58] that held that an *iniuria* is always subject to *de minimis non curat lex*. On the other hand there are two *iniuria* cases where the *de minimis* defence was unsuccessful, even though the infractions on these cases seem quite trivial. The first is *Communication Specialists CC v Poulter*,[59] where the appellant had written a letter to the respondent wherein it was stated that the respondent had acted deviously and reprehensively. On appeal the R3000 awarded as damages for *iniuria* was found to be excessive. The appeal court found that although his actions were not overly severe since the words were not published to anyone other than the respondent, it cannot be regarded as *de minimis* and the amount was reduced to R1000. In *Van Zyl v Marx* the appellant brought an action for *iniuria*,[60] claiming that his dignity had been injured when the respondent chased him out of his office after an argument regarding a tax certificate. At a later meeting where this

54 Para 71.

55 Para 213.

56 1958 3 SA 693 (SR) 695.

57 *De Lange v Costa* [1989] 2 All SA 267 (A).

58 (A217/11) 2012 ZAFSHC 79.

59 (CA 540/2002) 2003 ZAECHC 1.

60 (CA&R 109/2007) 2009 ZANCHC 62.

incident was discussed the respondent told the appellant *"As jy sê ek lieg, dan sê ek jy lieg ook"*.[61] In the trial court the respondent raised, among others, the defence of *de minimis non curat lex*. The trial court awarded damages of R300. The record of the appeal case consisted of seven volumes and 599 pages in total. According to Majiedt J, this was not a good reflection of the severity of the matter. There was no cross-appeal by the respondent, but the appeal court mentioned *obiter* that the *de minimis* defence should have been successful. In *Pharmavalu Sunnyside BK and Others v Pretorius*,[62] the appeal court found that the respondent had overreacted when he was suspected of taking something from the pharmacy without paying. It was found that he was denied an action for *iniuria* on grounds of the principle of *de minimis non curat lex*.

Much has changed since the *Walton* decision of 1958. The Constitution and the Equality Act now place a much higher premium on human dignity. The statement in *Walton* that minor or trivial insults to human dignity should be endured may therefore be frowned upon now by those who advocate for the proper validation of constitutional rights, such as human dignity. *Le Roux v Dey* seems to put the matter to rest, in any event, as the South African apex court vindicated a deputy principal's dignity in a case where many commentators would probably have reasoned that a harmless schoolboy prank should not warrant a court's attention.

(b) Section 10 of the Equality Act and the general characteristics of hate speech in terms of the *Qwelane* judgment

The Equality Act contains a civil prohibition of hate speech. The changes (strike-outs and insertions) to the original definition indicated below flow from *Qwelane*,[63] a Constitutional Court judgment where this court for the first time authoritatively interpreted section 10:

> 10. (1) Subject to the proviso in section 12, no person may publish, propagate, advocate or communicate words based on one or more of the prohibited grounds, against any person, that could reasonably be construed to demonstrate a clear intention to –
>
> a) ~~be hurtful~~;
>
> b) be harmful or to incite harm; *and*
>
> c) promote or propagate hatred.

61 "If you say I lied, then I say you lied too".

62 (A200/2009) [2010] ZAGPPHC 114.

63 *Qwelane v South African Human Rights Commission and Another* (CCT 13/20) [2021] ZACC 22; 2021 6 SA 579 (CC); 2022 2 BCLR 129 (CC).

> (2) Without prejudice to any remedies of a civil nature under this Act, the court may, in accordance with section 21(2)(*n*) and where appropriate, refer any case dealing with the publication, advocacy, propagation or communication of hate speech as contemplated in subsection (1), to the Director of Public Prosecutions having jurisdiction for the institution of criminal proceedings in terms of the common law or relevant legislation.
>
> 15. In cases of hate speech and harassment section 14 does not apply.

The impugned expression that formed the basis of the hate speech claim in *Qwelane* read as follows:

> The real problem, as I see it, is the rapid degradation of values and traditions by the so-called liberal influences of nowadays; you regularly see men kissing other men in public, walking holding hands and shamelessly flaunting what are misleadingly termed their 'lifestyle' and 'sexual preferences'. There could be a few things I could take issue with Zimbabwean President Robert Mugabe, but his unflinching and unapologetic stance over homosexuals is definitely not among those. Why, only this month – you'd better believe this – a man, in a homosexual relationship with another man, gave birth to a child! At least the so-called husband in that relationship hit the jackpot, making me wonder what it is these people have against the natural order of things. And by the way, please tell the Human Rights Commission that I totally refuse to withdraw or apologise for my views. ... Homosexuals and their backers will call me names, printable and not, for stating as I have always done my serious reservations about their lifestyle and sexual preferences, but quite frankly I don't give a damn: wrong is wrong. I do pray that someday a bunch of politicians with their heads affixed firmly to their necks will muster the balls to rewrite the Constitution of this country, to excise those sections which give license to men 'marrying' other men, and ditto women. Otherwise, at this rate, how soon before some idiot demands to 'marry' an animal, and argues that this Constitution 'allows' it.

The Constitutional Court identified the following general elements of hate speech. The Constitution protects equality, dignity, and freedom of expression equally (para 67). The expression of unpopular, repugnant, disturbing, offensive, or shocking ideas do not necessarily amount to hate speech (paras 74, 79, 81, 103). Merely hurtful words do not constitute hate speech (para 103). The difference between protected expression and hate speech is that while protected expression underpins a healthy democracy, hate speech destroys democracy (para 78). Hate speech is the severe loathing and disparagement of a vulnerable and marginalised group to the extent that it may lead to discrimination against that group (paras 81, 86). The target group's dignity and humanity and the "constitutional project of substantive equality and acceptance in [South African] society" must be undermined to constitute hate speech (para 130). Protection against hate speech is aimed at groups characterised by structural subordination, delegitimisation and rejection (paras 86, 103). The group must be subjected to hatred and the impugned expression must have the likely effect of maintaining negative stereotypes and unfair discrimination towards the group (para 118). Private communication is excluded (para 118). Factors to consider are the identity and status of the speaker, the context, the impact of the expression, and the likelihood of the expression causing harm and spreading hatred (para 176).

(c) *Qwelane*'s interpretation of section 10

In interpreting section 10 of the Equality Act specifically, the Court held as follows. Section 10 requires an abstract, objective reasonable person test; the test is not how a member of the target group could have interpreted the impugned expression but how a reasonable person would have received it, given the facts and circumstances in which the expression was made (paras 96, 100). This abstract reasonable person would not carry prejudices and would be cognisant of the diverse and dynamic South African society (para 100). Section 10(1)(a) falls away and section 10(1)(b) and (c) must be read conjunctively (paras 102, 154). Although section 10 refers to "words", it should be interpreted purposively to indicate that hate speech may consist of non-verbal expressions as well (paras 113, 115); the meaning behind the words is what a court should consider (para 115). "Words" should be read to refer to for example speech, ideas, ideologies, belief, meaning and instruction (para 115). It is not required to establish causation between the impugned expression and actual harm inflicted on the target group (paras 107, 110, 111); as long as the impugned expression at least arouses "a reasonable apprehension of harm to the target group" (para 112). "Harmful" in the context of section 10 should at a minimum be understood as "deep emotional and psychological harm that severely undermines the dignity of the targeted group" (para 154). A court may also consider the reactions of those who receive the impugned expression, are then fortified in their bigoted views and in turn also spurn, malign and abuse the target group (para 154); and may also consider the "harm to the social cohesion in South African society" (para 154). Although sexual orientation is not listed as one of the grounds in section 16(2) of the Constitution while it is listed in the Equality Act, this addition is a proportional limitation of the right to freedom of expression as the rights of sexual minorities cannot be protected without prohibiting hate speech based on sexual orientation (para 145).

In applying these guidelines to the impugned expression, the court held as follows. The published article expressed loathing and revulsion towards sexual minorities in four ways: (i) sexual minorities are responsible for the decline in South African morality; (ii) their sexual choices are unnatural and comparable to bestiality; (iii) they should not be allowed to marry; and (iv) South African law should not protect them (para 165). Unfair discrimination towards sexual minorities have been present in South Africa for centuries (para 168). South Africa's transformative Constitution demands that the remains of South Africa's colonial and apartheid heritage must be eradicated (para 168). Identity and status of the speaker: the perpetrator was an experienced journalist and struggle veteran with a loyal following in Black townships (para 177). Context: The article approved of former president Mugabe's notorious remarks about sexual minorities at a time when significantly violent attacks against this community was taking place (and is still taking place) (para 178). Impact of the expression: The article contained explicit, undiluted denigration and disparagement of the community. After the publication, the SAHRC and the Press Ombud were flooded by complaints. Ms MN testified during the original trial that South African law does not care about them and that she has suffered from unrelenting physical attacks and vilification, based on their sexual orientation. Ms MN testified that she felt that she had "died inside" (para 179). There is a strong correlation between the occurrence and acceptance of hate speech, and the occurrence of hate crimes against vulnerable groups (para 180). Likelihood of harm and hatred: The target group's dignity was devastatingly maligned by a seasoned journalist in a publication with a significant circulation. The target group was harmed, and the South African constitutional project was harmed as the publication was antithetical to the values of equality, dignity and acceptance (para 181).

(d) Criticisms of the *Qwelane* judgment

There are some unfortunate and puzzling aspects to the *Qwelane* ruling. We list five criticisms below. Firstly, as a matter of logical semantics, it does not make sense to read sections 10(1)(a) to (c) conjunctively. An expression that promotes or propagates *hatred* is obviously also *harmful* and *hurtful*. An expression that is harmful or incites harm, is obviously hurtful – the court admits as much in paragraph 155. For subsections (a) and (b) to play a meaningful role in section 10(1), they should logically be self-standing provisions, not connected to each other. So, subsections (a) to (c) should be read as progressively worse categories of objectionable expression – either hurtful *or* harmful *or* hatred-filled expression. If the three requirements are to be read conjunctively, there would not have been any need to include the requirements listed in (a) and (b) as words that promote or propagate hatred would obviously also be harmful and hurtful. The High Court judgment in *Herselman* captures our argument:[64]

> If one has regard to the purpose of the Act and the interpretation clause it militates against the acceptance of the conjunctive approach. If one were to adopt a conjunctive approach then racially discriminatory words which are clearly hurtful and even harmful, which are directed at an individual may not fall within the ambit of the Act simply because they may not *per se* promote or propagate hatred … This is untenable and could not have been the intention of the legislature.

Secondly, the court recognised section 10 as creating a statutory tort (para 95). In South African law, the *actio iniuriarum* is a common law tort that protects the infringement of the plaintiff's reputation and dignity. In *Le Roux v Dey*, the same apex court held that the *actio iniuriarum* is constitutional, in its form of the wrongful, intentional infringement of the plaintiff's reputation or dignity. In *Qwelane*, the court held that the qualifier "hurtful" is vague and redundant (para 155). However, in *Le Roux* the same court had no difficulty in interpreting the same qualifier, in the same context – a tort that protects dignity. *Le Roux* is replete with explanations of how "hurtful" should be understood – "insulting", "offensive", "degrading" (para 113); "belittling", "making the plaintiff look foolish and unworthy of respect", "exposing the plaintiff to ridicule and contempt" (para 114; 115); would the impugned expression humiliate or demean the plaintiff (para 116); a value judgment should be made to consider if the plaintiff is presented as foolish, ridiculous or unworthy of respect (para 119); "humiliation and ridicule" (para 132); "wounded feelings" (para 142); and an injury to the plaintiff's own sense of self-worth (para 154). So, on the one hand, *Le Roux* holds that a civil claim exists in South African *common law* for offensive expression. On the other hand, *Qwelane* holds that a civil claim does *not* exist in South African *statutory law* for offensive expression.

Curiously, the Constitutional Court held in *Qwelane* that the word "hurtful" be excised from the Act. We now have the untenable position in South African law that ordinary insults, whether committed in private or in the public arena, are actionable in the ordinary South African courts, based on the hurt caused to the plaintiff, but insults based on the prohibited grounds must be committed in public and must be (i) harmful or incite harm; and (ii) promote or propagate hatred, to be actionable in the equality courts. *Qwelane* read with *Le Roux* is incoherent and illogical.

64 *Herselman v Geleba* (231/2009) [2011] ZAECGHC 108 18.

In the third place, *Qwelane* held that section 10 of the Equality Act does not apply to private communications (paras 102, 116, 118). On the other hand, the *actio iniuriarum* for insult applies to private communications, as the claim *inter alia* consists of the infringement of the plaintiff's subjective right to dignity, for which no third party hearing the communication is required. (In *De Lange v Costa*,[65] for example, the communication was contained in a letter that only the plaintiff read.)

Fourthly, *Qwelane* further held that if section 10 hate speech claims had to be founded on the speaker's subjective intention, "the threshold for civil liability would be considerably higher than usual" (para 99). It is not clear what the court is referring to here, as the "usual civil liability" standard is precisely the speaker's subjective intention in terms of the *actio iniuriarum*.

In the fifth place, section 15 of the Equality Act states that a defence of "fair" hate speech is untenable. After the *Qwelane* judgment, section 15 of the Equality Act does not seem to carry any meaning anymore, as the various factors that the court identified in considering if a claim for hate speech has been established, boils down to a "fairness" enquiry. Legal interpretation of laws should not lead to a particular statutory provision becoming superfluous. Nowhere in *Qwelane* does the court deal with or refer to section 15.

The Constitutional Court should have harmonised the definition of hate speech in the Equality Act and the common law *actio iniuriarum* and should have kept the qualifier "hurtful" intact in section 10 of the Equality Act. We set out in this paragraph our imagined (and better) application of section 10, as if *Qwelane* does not apply. For hate speech claims, the objective "reasonable person" test would play a different role than for common law claims based on intentional insults. For hate speech cases, the emphasis should not be on preventing courts from being flooded with so-called trivial claims. The reason for insisting on a reasonable person element for the test for hate speech should be to ensure that a value-laden enquiry takes place, and that important and difficult conversations are not shut down for fear of being labelled as hate speech.[66]

65 *De Lange v Costa* [1989] 2 All SA 267 (A).

66 *South African Human Rights Commission v Khumalo* 2019 1 SA 289 (GJ) para 92: "[I]t is the reasonable reader's understanding of the effect of the utterances that forms the substance of the test. The category of reasonable reader is not confined to being a member of the group being vilified; reasonable people anywhere and everywhere are envisaged …". *Herselman v Geleba* (231/2009) [2011] ZAECGHC 108 24 gets it wrong where the court suggests that "it would be impossible to determine the reasonable man in South African context having regard to the number of languages and different race groups in South Africa". The reasonable person who is imagined here is an ideal type to concretise the test for what would constitute hurt. *Herselman* 25 is closer to what is imagined here:

Words that are derogatory, insulting, demeaning, or stigmatising, based on one or more of the prohibited grounds, should ordinarily meet the requirement of being "hurtful" and should ordinarily amount to hate speech; no matter the race or gender or other characteristics of the speaker or the receiver of the message. However, robust conversations on, for example, the socio-economic conditions of the majority of South Africans and the historical causes of this condition (colonialism, conquest, apartheid, homophobia, and the like) should ordinarily not constitute hate speech. The line dividing permissible from impermissible speech will not always be easy to draw. For hate speech complaints that draw directly from our painful past and its ongoing consequences in a deeply unequal society, courts should pay particular attention to the remedy to be awarded, considering the purpose of the Equality Act. We part ways here to some extent with what was said in *South African Human Rights Commission v Khumalo*:[67]

> Our nation-building project recognises a multitude of justifiable grievances derived from past oppression and racial domination. The value choice in the Constitution is that we must overcome the fissures among us. That cannot happen if, in debate, however robust, among ourselves, one section of the population is licensed to be condemnatory because its members were the victims of oppression, and the other section, understood to be, collectively, the former oppressors is disciplined to remain silent.

In our view we can only overcome the fissures among us if we have honest and painful conversations, and a notional reasonable person would appreciate this and would allow for some leeway in these conversations. No one should be asked to remain silent, but we should remain respectful of one another while having robust and painful and deeply uncomfortable conversations. The concern in *Khumalo* seems to be with talk of violence against whites. Khumalo was rightly found to have committed hate speech – he said that whites deserved to be hacked and killed like Jews and they must be burned alive and skinned. Of course, the oppressed majority in South Africa "is licensed to be

"the fictitious normal, balanced, orthodox and reasonable person who is neither hypercritical nor oversensitive". Some equality courts, pre-*Qwelane*, devised a test for establishing "hurt" by asking what the target audience of the slur would have experienced (as for example in *Afriforum v Malema* 2010 5 SA 235 (GNP) 237E, 239H–I, 240B–D and 240F: "what is the effect of the words, objectively considered, on those directly affected and targeted thereby?"). This test has now been discarded in favour of an objective "reasonable person" test.

67 2019 1 SA 289 (GJ) para 102.

condemnatory" – how else can we deal with our painful past? There are of course limits to how this condemnation should be expressed – and these limits should be drawn by a fictional reasonable person, properly appraised of the Constitution and the Equality Act, and Khumalo clearly crossed the limit. The application of this "reasonable person" test must be done with particular care. Given South Africa's tortuous past, this reasonable person cannot be blind to past and present forms of marginalisation and victimisation based on prohibited grounds such as race, class, sexual orientation, gender identify and gender expression. If misapplied, sexual minority litigants may for example be told that they are being oversensitive, that they should let it go – while real hurt occurred. The Equality Act in effect creates legislated torts of unfair discrimination, harassment and hate speech. The Bill of Rights contains justiciable human rights to dignity and freedom of expression. The common law personality right to human dignity is now also a human right. The protection of the right to dignity has now been further fleshed out in the Equality Act in the creation of a legislated tort of hate speech. The definition of hate speech in the Equality Act is broad and should be carefully delineated to give proper protection to the right to dignity while at the same time not to unduly limit freedom of expression. The intention of the legislature to facilitate societal transformation should also be given effect to. Section 39(2) of the Constitution compels courts to interpret the qualifier "hurtful" by taking all of these considerations into account. The existing common law "reasonable person" test, with slight adaptation, seems to be a workable and sensible method of properly balancing dignity and freedom of expression: Would a reasonable person "properly apprised of constitutional values and the aim of the Equality Act" also have felt insulted in the same circumstances?

As a postscript to this section, relying on *Qwelane*, the Supreme Court of Appeal in *Afriforum v Economic Freedom Fighters and others*,[68] held that the somewhat controversial struggle chant "kill/shoot the boer" is not hate speech. Very briefly summarised, the Supreme Court of Appeal held that the words used in this struggle song would not be interpreted literally by the notional reasonable person, but would be understood in its historical context, and that a reasonable person would understand that if this song is sung in present circumstances, it is *inter alia* a call for an end to economic and land injustice. Whether the judgment is correct or not, the implications for the creation of a kind and caring South African society are somewhat problematic. If the Constitution and the Equality Act are seen as the "moderator's handbook" of the national conversation, it is not self-evident why disrespectful, disparaging,

68 [2024] ZASCA 82, 2024 6 SA 1 (SCA).

offensive and shocking speech should be tolerated. A "healthy democratic dialogue" must be uncomfortable to be productive; the dialogue should provoke the participants to think deeper, reflect, and adjust their positions and attitudes. Speech that is offensive and shocking is too easy to dismiss or may lead to hardening attitudes on the side of the targets of such speech, or may lead to retaliatory offence, and probably then leaves no room for cognitive empathy to emerge.

(e) Post-*Qwelane* reasoning

How should South African courts now deal with derogatory slurs, after *Qwelane*?

In *Thembani v Swanepoel*, the respondent was held to have committed hate speech in terms of section 10 of the Equality Act when he uttered the vile racial slur "kaffir".[69] The judgment was handed down before *Qwelane*, and aspects of the judgment are no longer good law. *Qwelane* held that "hurtful" be excised from section 10 and that the remaining two qualifiers be read conjunctively. *Thembani* (para 11) still applied the qualifier "hurtful" and read the three qualifiers disjunctively. *Qwelane* held that an objective approach be adopted when applying section 10; *Thembani* (paras 11–12) somewhat contradictory held that an objective approach should be adopted but then considered that "a reasonable *African person* would ... consider the use of this word under the circumstances as derogatory and constituting hate speech" (emphasis added). *Thembani* (para 13) further held that the slur is derogatory, abusive, disparaging and contemptuous of the person to which it is aimed. The court held that the slur is hurtful and that it promotes hatred (para 13); for whatever reason not holding that the slur is harmful.

In *Herselman v Geleba* the court had to consider if the word "baboon" said by a white man to a black man constituted meaningless abuse – *de minimis non curat lex* by another name. The court held that the circumstances in which the word was uttered, the context in which it was used, the tone in which it was uttered, and the effect of the words, objectively considered, on those directly affected and targeted are relevant. In the South African context, the use of the word "baboon" is racially charged. It has a derogatory meaning and would be construed as such by any reasonable African person.[70] The court therefore held that hate speech in terms of section 10 of the Equality Act had been committed – presumably on the basis that the word was hurtful. Post-*Qwelane*, how should such slurs be adjudicated?

69 *Thembani v Swanepoel* 2017 3 SA 70 (ECM).

70 *Herselman v Geleba* (231/2009) [2011] ZAECGHC 108 21–25.

In our view derogatory slurs directed towards vulnerable groups, such as sexual and gender minorities, as for the "k" word, should still constitute hate speech in terms of section 10 of the Equality Act, but this conclusion is open to some doubt. It is not self-evident that a court will consider the "k" word and slurs against sexual minorities as equally vile, or the "k" word and a slur such as "baboon" as equally vile. The *Qwelane* court was called upon to interpret a newspaper column where the author denigrated sexual minorities in multiple sentences. Will a future court hold that an abusive, one word, slur against sexual minorities does the same work? On a strict literal reading of *Thembani*, remembering that for a slur to constitute hate speech, the two qualifiers have to be read conjunctively, the "k" word is not hate speech, as the court did not hold that the "k" word is harmful. In a post-*Qwelane* setting however, *Thembani* is likely to be read as the larger sin (promoting hatred) obviously including the lesser sin (being harmful). Whereas the "k" word is aimed at the majority of the South African population, slurs against sexual minorities are aimed at a politically vulnerable group, a group of which members are exposed to the risk of death and rape and other extreme forms of marginalisation and exclusion.

Why the *Qwelane* judgment is particularly disappointing is that section 10 hate speech claims may be brought to equality courts, by filling in a form at the clerk's office and without the assistance of a lawyer. Because "hurtful" words and actions no longer constitute hate speech, these actions would in future have to be brought in terms of the common law *actio iniuriarum*, in the ordinary courts, with the assistance of a lawyer. The Equality Act envisages equality courts as vehicles for social transformation and for creating a kind and caring South African society. *Qwelane* implicitly holds that (equality) courts are not made for this purpose.

(f) A proposed legislative response to *Qwelane*

It is open to the South African Parliament to respond to *Qwelane* and make another attempt to outlaw insulting speech by mirroring the *actio iniuriarum* in a legislated tort. The *actio iniuriarum* has been given the green light by the Constitutional Court in *Le Roux v Dey*, so to mirror this common law action in legislation should not pose difficulty. A legislated tort of "insult" could, for example, be phrased as follows:

> **10 Civil prohibition of insult**
>
> (1) This section creates a constitutional delict (civil cause of action) termed 'insult'.

(2) No person may wrongfully and intentionally insult another person, by their words or conduct,[71] based on one or more of the prohibited grounds.

(3) If the insult was not based on one or more of the prohibited grounds, the common law applies.

(4) The complainant must establish that

(a) subjectively, their dignity was violated; and

(b) objectively, a reasonable person, properly apprised of constitutional values and the aim of this Act, would also have been hurt in the same circumstances.

(5) A respondent may raise any of the following defences to a claim based on this section:

(a) lack of intention to insult the complainant (*animus iniuriandi*); or

(b) *bona fide* engagement in artistic creativity; or

(c) *bona fide* academic or scientific inquiry; or

(d) fair and accurate reporting in the public interest; or

(e) any of the common law defences that are available to a defendant in a common law claim based on insult, subject to section 39(2) of the Constitution of the Republic of South Africa, 1996.

This legislated tort of insult would largely mirror the common law *actio iniuriarum*, with the added qualifier that the insult be related to a prohibited ground, to fit within the scheme of the rest of the Equality Act. Including this tort in the Equality Act has the added benefit that a complainant may then approach an inexpensive and informal equality court, and initiate the claim by filling in a form at the court in their home language, without the assistance of a lawyer. If only the *actio iniuriarum* is available to complainants, a lawyer would be required to initiate the claim and draft the pleadings in an ordinary (much more expensive) magistrate's or High Court.

To meet the requirements of the Constitutional Court in *Le Roux v Dey*, the fault requirement would have to be set as intent (*dolus*). The definition of micro-aggressions by Sue et al, that a micro-aggression does not have to be perpetrated intentionally or consciously and that the "offender" does not have to be purposefully hostile,[72] will have to be restricted in South African law to intentional insults. However, South African law recognises constructive intent (*dolus eventualis*): if the wrongdoer subjectively foresees that the plaintiff

71 The qualifier "conduct" is intended to cover the expansive interpretation given to the qualifier "words" in *Qwelane* para 115 to include, for example, "ideas, ideologies, belief, meaning, instructions".

72 Sue *et al* (2007) 62 *American Psychologist* 271 274.

could or would be insulted by their conduct but, regardless of that foresight, proceeds with the insult (reconciles themself with this possibility), intent will be present.[73] Findings of guilt on a criminal charge of *crimen iniuria* based on *dolus eventualis* have been made in South African courts.[74] By analogy the same finding would follow in a civil suit based on the *actio iniuriarum* or a legislated tort of insult.

73 *S v Steenberg* 1999 1 SACR 594 (N) 597E–G.

74 Eg *Steenberg* ibid and *S v Van der Merwe* 2011 2 SACR 509 (FB).

CHAPTER 7

Ways Forward for Addressing Micro-aggressions

In this final chapter, we aim to chart a way forward for national legislatures on how to address micro-aggressions. One option is to explicitly proclaim that freedom of expression yields before dignity and substantive equality, by for example creating a statutory tort of "insult", as set out above. This approach does not seem to carry much favour anywhere, however. Another option would be to promote the ideal and inherent values of substantive equality, respect and kindness through national action plans, and the monitoring and enforcement of these plans through well-resourced, committed and wise bureaucrats and judges. We make a case for the abandonment of *de minimis* in cases involving micro-aggressions against vulnerable groups in Section 1 below, and explain how mandated equality action plans, *inter alia*, could address micro-aggressions in Section 2 below.

1 Discard *de minimis non curat lex* Where Micro-aggressions Occur against Vulnerable Groups

We argued that the qualifiers contained in the causes of action recognised in the South African Equality Act should be interpreted purposively and generously to achieve the Equality Act's purpose and not be used to dismiss seemingly trivial instances of discrimination, hate speech and harassment. Deeply ingrained discrimination does not disappear overnight, and attitudes do not change swiftly. The Equality Act's aim of large-scale societal transformation will inevitably be hindered if courts brand discrimination as trivial (and therefore find that the impugned discrimination was fair); if courts brand insulting words and conduct as trivial (and therefore find that the words did not constitute hate speech); and if courts brand demeaning conduct as trivial (and therefore find that the harassment was not serious and that the claim fails).

Section 24 of the Equality Act provides that it is the duty of the state and all persons to promote equality. If "trivial" instances of discrimination, hate speech and harassment are tolerated in South African society, it exposes a disregard for this responsibility. The failure to hold perpetrators accountable in these instances arguably increase the likelihood of infringements in the future.

South Africa's past is characterised by many violations of human rights and profuse social, economic and political inequality, and the new constitutional

 | HTTPS://DOI.ORG/10.1163/9789004757523-008

order attempts to remedy the lingering effects of these evils. When ostensibly "trivial" incidents attack important values or threaten an escalation of harms, the law should concern itself with these infractions, because these seemingly small violations are not giving effect to the promotion of equality and progressive change as described in the Equality Act. Continual awareness and adamant enforcement are of utmost importance when attempting to protect constitutional rights. The equality courts are therefore tailor-made to address the "daily pinpricks, the little discourtesies, the minute humiliations".[1]

In light of the South African Constitution and the objective of transformation,[2] the question arises whether the maxim of *de minimis non curat lex* also applies in cases of discrimination, hate speech and harassment in terms of the Equality Act. In this regard, it is important to consider the above-mentioned factor usually considered when determining whether the maxim of *de minimis* should be applied, namely the objective of the specific rule or statute, and whether its application would frustrate the purpose of the obligation in question.[3] It can be said that an action will be considered to be *de minimis* when it does not cause the harm sought to be prevented by the particular law.[4]

The achievement of (substantive) equality is a constitutional imperative and is part of the broader project aimed at the transformation of South African society.[5] The Constitution instructs us to strive for a society built on the democratic values of human dignity, the achievement of equality and freedom.[6] As pointed out by Langa J, the notion of transformation plays a vital role in interpreting the Constitution.[7] The concept of transformation can be described as "mandating the achievement of substantive equality and social justice, the infiltration of human rights norms into private relationships and the fostering of a 'culture of justification' for every exercise of public power".[8]

Because the violation of fundamental rights often goes unremedied without the use of *de minimis*, no wrongdoing concerning human rights should

1 Tutu (1999) 74.
2 The preamble of the South African Constitution lists the healing of the divisions of the past and establishing a society based on democratic values as objectives of the Constitution. The preamble of the South African Equality Act also sets out as one of the Act's aims the transition to a democratic society.
3 *Wisconsin Department of Revenue v William Wrigley Jr Co* 505 U.S. 1992 214 232; Hoctor (2012) 80 *e-Mantshi* 9 11.
4 Rank (2005–2006) 36 *Seton Hall Law Review* 223 242.
5 Woolman & Bishop (2014) Chapter 35.1 OS 03–07 1.
6 *Minister of Finance v Van Heerden* 2004 6 SA 121 (CC) para 22.
7 Langa (2006) 17 *Stellenbosch Law Review* 351.
8 Pieterse (2005) 20 *Southern African Public Law* 155.

ever be regarded as a trifle.[9] Since the addressing of smaller violations can limit the encouragement of worse behaviour, it warrants recognition.[10] In "The Nature of Prejudice"[11] the psychologist Allport explains that there are five stages of discrimination, namely hate speech, avoidance, concrete actions of discrimination, physical attack and finally extermination. It is consequently clear that discrimination usually starts with something trivial and escalates to something greater. The same theory was confirmed by an experiment whereby it was established that participants were less likely to contribute financially to a women's organisation after exposure to sexist humour.[12] Discrimination and harassment may often, especially on grounds of sexual orientation, escalate to physical violence or crime if left unresolved.[13] Some even opine that the moderate and light invasions of constitutional rights are the most dangerous.[14] Already in the 1800s, an American court made the following statement:

> It may be that it is the obnoxious thing in its mildest and least repulsive form; but illegitimate and unconstitutional practices get their first footing in that way, namely, by silent approaches and slight deviations from legal modes of procedure ... It is the duty of courts to be watchful for the constitutional rights of the citizen, and against any stealthy encroachments thereon. Their motto should be *obsia principiis*.[15]

The antithesis is also true. Since small things can grow bigger in the right contextual soil,[16] a relatively small public display of progress (eg a new gay-straight alliance in a school or an intervention that makes life in public spaces easier for a person with a disability) can generate relatively large improvements[17] whereby equality can be promoted.

In *Director of Public Prosecutions, Eastern Cape v Klue*[18] the acquittal on the basis of *de minimis* in the court *a quo* on a charge of driving with excessive alcohol in the blood was overturned. The court held that in the light of the carnage on the roads and the section prohibiting driving under the influence of

9 Bernstein (2010) 62 *Florida Law Review* 895 899.
10 Ibid 900.
11 Allport (1979) 52.
12 Ford *et al* (2007) 34 *Personality & Social Psychology Bulletin* 159.
13 Bernstein (2010) 62 *Florida Law Review* 895 917.
14 Guthrie (1898) 40.
15 *Boyd v United States* 116 U.S. 616 (1886).
16 Coldwell (2009) *Financial Times*.
17 Bernstein (2010) 62 *Florida Law Review* 895 949.
18 2003 1 SACR 389 (E).

intoxicating liquor,[19] there was no room for the application of the *de minimis* defence in this context. It was also mentioned that nothing but good would come if no one drank alcohol before driving and that the permitted blood alcohol limit is a concession to a pernicious practice, which ought not to be further extended by judicial discretion.[20] The court held that "where the Legislature has determined a statutory limit, there is no room for the application of the *de minimis* rule where the limit is exceeded. In a sense, the Legislature has already determined what would be regarded as negligible, and it is not for the Courts to raise that limit".[21] This sentiment was expressed in relation to a minimum blood alcohol level but the same considerations should apply where the Legislature has set a minimum statutory threshold for the application of the Equality Act – if the requirements are present, the Act should apply and a remedy should be ordered – the more so given the importance of the right to substantive equality in the 1996 Constitution, and the express purpose of the Equality Act to facilitate the creation of a caring South African society.

The same consideration as expressed in *Klue* should apply in terms of the Equality Act, since nothing but good would come if a zero-tolerance policy regarding discrimination could be established, especially in the context of South Africa's history and the desired transformation. As Webster J stated in *S v Seweya*: "It is regrettable that some members of society may still cling to stereotyping people or harbour idiosyncrasies of sexual superiority or inferiority or believe in some form of domination or quaint local unwritten rules or cultural practices".[22]

The Equality Act is explicitly ambitious and set up precisely to facilitate transformation. It should thus be read and interpreted in this way.[23] It is often in the minutiae of daily interactions where we create a sense of belonging or alienation, and it is precisely here where the equality courts can play some role – especially while the chapter in the Equality Act on the promotion of equality is not yet in force.

19 National Road Traffic Act 93 of 1996, sec 65.

20 Hoctor (2012) 80 *e-Mantshi* 9 12.

21 Para 13.

22 2004 1 SACR 387 (T) 392.

23 For an opposite result, see Ross-Amato (2002–2003) 29 *William Mitchell Law Review* 569 who discusses the outcome of *Goins v West Group Inc* – the Minnesota Supreme Court's first interpretation of discrimination against transgender people. The author shows how the court felt that that "society is not yet prepared for and the Minnesota legislature had not anticipated a means of restroom designation based on self-image ... Unless the legislature has expressly considered and accounted for such implications, the court would not interpret a statute to create a result with such broad implications".

Deeply ingrained discrimination does not disappear overnight, and attitudes do not change swiftly.[24] The ultimate objective of transformation will inevitably be hindered if judicial discretion allows for instances of discrimination and describes these as "trivial" or, even worse, "fair" discrimination.

The Equality Act contains a provision that it is the duty of the state and all persons to promote equality.[25] If discrimination is at all tolerated in a society, it exposes a disregard for this responsibility. Failure to adjudicate these violations will increase the likelihood of infringements in the future.[26]

South Africa's past is characterised by many violations of human rights and profuse social, economic and political inequality, and the constitutional order attempts to remedy the lingering effects of these evils.[27] When trivial things attack important values or threaten escalation of harms,[28] the law should concern itself therewith, because these small violations are not giving effect to the promotion of equality and progressive change as described in the Equality Act.[29] Continual awareness and adamant enforcement are of utmost importance when attempting to protect constitutional rights.[30] The equality courts therefore seem tailor made to address the "daily pinpricks, the little discourtesies, the minute humiliations".[31]

Whether *de minimis* should be invoked or not, is a value judgment;[32] rather ironically expressed in an offensive statement in *R v Maguire*:[33] "slaps delivered by fishwives to each other during a drunken brawl might well be ignored on the principle of *de minimis non curat lex* whereas an unprovoked slap delivered to the face of a lady, say at a garden party, could not be similarly ignored". This value judgment includes a proper weighing up of the interests of the community as

---

24 Pieterse (2000) 16 *South African Journal on Human Rights* 121 137.

25 Sec 24.

26 Inest (2006) 21 *Berkeley Technology Law Journal* 945 959.

27 Pieterse (2000) 16 *South African Journal on Human Rights* 121.

28 Bernstein (2010) 62 *Florida Law Review* 895 949.

29 Sec 3.

30 Guthrie (1898) 41.

31 Tutu (1999) 74. Also see Bohler (2000) 63 *Journal of Contemporary Roman-Dutch Law* 288 and Bohler-Muller (2000) 16 *South African Journal on Human Rights* 623. Labuschagne (1973) *Acta Juridica* 291 304 argues for the creation of small claims courts for torts and contractual claims (in the context of an article on *de minimis non curat lex*). The equality courts are in effect small claims courts for the legislated torts of unfair discrimination, hate speech and harassment.

32 *S v Visagie* 2009 2 SACR 70 (W) para 15. Arguably, the fact that the application of the maxim amounts to a value judgment, is why "the cases in which *de minimis* is used cannot ... be readily reconciled" – Veech & Moon (1947) 45 *Michigan Law Review* 537 544.

33 1969 4 SA 191 (RA) 195A–C.

a whole.[34] The Equality Act concretises these community interests. The Act was put in place to bring section 9(4) of the 1996 Constitution into life. What is expressed in two sentences in section 9(4) of the 1996 Constitution is fleshed out in considerable detail – who may claim against whom, for which causes of action, to which ends – large-scale and significant societal transformation.

The available remedies listed in the Equality Act should also be taken as a directive to equality courts to use these to further the aims of the Act (and the Constitution, who gave life to the Equality Act). If one of the aims of the Equality Act is to create a caring society, and if one of the "daily pinpricks" should feature in an equality court case, the presiding officer should consider which remedy(ies) will have the best chance at rehabilitating the respondent and preventing further infractions, either by the respondent or other potential violators. In South African law, the monetary awards paid out in cases of personality harm is done so to compensate the plaintiff for hurt feelings.[35] However it also has a penal function.[36] Such payments may therefore act as a deterrent.[37]

One of the ostensible reasons for recognising the maxim is to avoid wasting courts' valuable time.[38] But the application of the maxim sees courts spend considerable time on considering if the maxim should be applied – see *S v Visagie* as a recent example where the court goes into great detail comparing the facts of the dispute against previous cases.[39] The assumption then seems to be that legal practitioners and prosecutors must take their cue from the few reported judgments on the maxim and exercise their discretion in avoiding prosecutions for trivial offences, or to advise clients to let trivial disputes be. What we do not know is how many lawyers advise their clients not to approach an equality court; not to approach their HR division; not to make a fuss; or if complainants themselves question whether what happened to them was really discrimination, hate speech, harassment; and decide not take it further; or how many equality court clerks advise complainants not to pursue the claim as the clerk perceive the matter as frivolous.

34 *S v Visagie* 2009 2 SACR 70 (W) para 16.

35 Neethling (2005) 38 *Comparative and International Law Journal of Southern Africa* 220 222.

36 Ibid.

37 Ibid.

38 *S v Visagie* 2009 2 SACR 70 (W) para 36; Nemerofsky (2001–2002) 37 *Gonzaga Law Review* 315 324.

39 Also see Veech & Moon (1947) 45 *Michigan Law Review* 537 538: "Actually, in every case in which the *de minimis* maxim is cited or applied, the law is *concerning* itself with what is found to be or alleged to be a trifle".

The causes of action created in the Equality Act strike at the core of injuries caused by centuries of colonialism, patriarchy, apartheid and other forms of oppression. The reasons sometimes given for recognising *de minimis* – ignoring small and intangible injuries as part of the price of living in society, to prevent expensive and mischievous litigation that cannot result in any real benefit to the complainant – simply do not apply when the Equality Act is operative.[40] These daily pinpricks are exactly what the Equality Act sets itself up against.[41] The litigation need not be expensive at all – complainants and respondents alike may appear before the equality courts without legal representation and claims are instituted by completing a form, not by issuing a summons and particulars of claim in legalese. The benefit to the complainant and to society at large is to vindicate the denial of dignity.

Another reason to avoid *de minimis* in cases dealing with the Equality Act is that it will reduce courts' accountability towards the South African (legal) community. Reasons should be given and judgments explained with recourse to principles. The qualifiers in the Equality Act itself – "unfair", "persistent", "serious", "hurtful" – should be used to justify a particular finding; not recourse to some general observation on a particular claim being too trifle to engage with.

It should in most cases not be difficult to distinguish between hate speech and harassment on the one hand, and a *bona fide* uncomfortable conversation on the other hand. In cases of doubt, should such a matter end up in an equality court, the presiding officer should take particular care to vindicate the parties' dignity, but at the same time craft a remedy that will not stifle debate on difficult societal issues. To experience discomfort when a difficult conversation is taking place on social justice is not the same as being hurt.[42] To be quite blunt: If a black South African tells a white South African that his ancestors stole the land, it is an uncomfortable truth but not hurtful. Likewise, if that white South African tells the black South African that taxpayers' money is being squandered on corrupt politicians' deals instead of being used optimally for the upliftment of previously disadvantaged groups, it may be

40 Compare Nemerofsky (2001–2002) 37 *Gonzaga Law Review* 315 323–324.

41 I therefore agree with how Nemerofksy puts it at 331: "Some courts hold that constitutional rights are so sacred in our system of justice that they can never be compromised, regardless of how small the deprivation". In South Africa's justiciable Bill of Rights, the right to substantive equality is the prime right and should not be compromised.

42 We would therefore prefer to talk of "brave spaces" instead of "safe spaces" – a space for an uncomfortable conversation but not an insulting or degrading conversation. See eg Landreman (2013) 135 and further; Holley & Steiner (2005) 1 *Journal of Social Work Education* 49.

uncomfortable to hear but is not hurtful. If the white South African is told that he is no longer welcome in the country and should leave, or if the black South African is told that all black politicians are corrupt, a line is crossed and such utterances should be sanctioned. Such unacceptable utterances should not be conversation stoppers however.

Lastly: not only courts; the court of public opinion and other forums are also of some import. There may well be a radiating effect of anti-marginalisation norms as they appear in domestic constitutions and legislation. What may have been shrugged off as trivialities in the past is now taken very seriously indeed in various jurisdictions, and rightly so.[43] (However, we should note that public opinion and politicians can be capricious – small indignities are not in all cases being targeted appropriately.[44])

2 Promote the Values of Substantive Equality, Kindness and Respect in Equality Plans

If the argument in favour of courts acting as "hearts and minds" transformers is unpersuasive or seems draconian or impractical, how else may national legislatures aim to create kinder, more inclusive and diverse societies be realised? We refer to the South African model in this section, but the approach suggested here could be sensibly applied anywhere.

The chapter in the Equality Act that deals with the promotion of equality – the part that directly addresses changes in hearts and minds – is not in force yet. Chapter 5 of the Equality Act, in its current form, presupposes that the model to be followed when concretising the duty to promote equality is that of prescribing equality plans and action plans and having these plans submitted to a monitoring body. To operationalise this chapter in the Equality Act, regulations would have to be effected to make provision for equality plans, action

43 For a few examples from the popular media, see https://www.theguardian.com/sport/2019/apr/11/israel-folau-to-be-sacked-by-rugby-australia-over-social-media-posts?CMP=Share_iOSApp_Other (accessed 5 September 2025); https://www.theguardian.com/commentisfree/2019/apr/02/joe-biden-inapprorpriate-touching-lucy-flores?CMP=Share_iOSApp_Other (accessed 5 September 2025); https://www.vox.com/policy-and-politics/2019/3/29/18241598/joe-biden-lucy-flores-touching-women-media-history-explained (accessed 5 September 2025); https://edition.cnn.com/2019/04/12/uk/upskirting-uk-criminal-offense-intl-scli-gbr/ (accessed 5 September 2025); https://www.bbc.com/news/world-europe-48104247 (accessed 5 September 2025).

44 Eg https://www.theguardian.com/world/2019/may/01/have-you-heard-about-the-philippine-mayor-who-banned-gossip?CMP=Share_iOSApp_Other (accessed 5 September 2025).

plans, the monitoring of these plans and some enforcement mechanism if plans are neither drafted nor implemented.

Draft regulations dealing with the promotion of equality in the general sense have been published for comment,[45] but have not yet been given legal effect. The regulations distinguish between the promotion of equality by the state, and the promotion of equality by "all persons". As to the state's obligations, the regulations envisage the drafting of equality plans by state departments.[46] These plans must be drafted for a five-year period. These plans must then be submitted to the South African Human Rights Commission (SAHRC), which in turn must submit the plan to the Commission for Gender Equality (CGE) for purposes of consultation. The SAHRC is a national institution created by Chapter 9 of the Constitution. Section 184 of the Constitution sets out the mandate of the SAHRC which states that the SAHRC must promote respect for human rights and a culture of human rights; promote the protection, development and attainment of human rights; and monitor and assess the observance of human rights in the Republic. Therefore, the role assigned to the SAHRC by the draft regulations falls squarely within the mandate of the SAHRC. In terms of the draft regulations, the SAHRC must consider and assess each of these equality plans, make appropriate recommendations to the relevant state department and report to the National Assembly in terms of Section 181(5) of the Constitution. (Section 181(5) states that Chapter 9 institutions are accountable to the National Assembly.) In terms of the draft regulations, each state department must also submit annual progress reports to the SAHRC, which must then assess each of these progress reports and if, necessary, must advise the relevant departments on measures to be put in place to expedite the implementation of the equality plan.[47]

As to the promotion of equality by "all persons", section 28 of the draft regulations distinguishes between "entities" that employ more than 150 employees, more than 50 but less than 150 employees and less than 50 employees. Entities that employ more than 150 employees must submit equality plans to the Director-General of the Department of Justice and Constitutional Development. These plans are valid for five years. Annual progress reports must also be submitted to the Department. The Director-General then forwards the plans to the appropriate national state department and that department then analyses the plans. The progress reports are dealt with on a similar basis. Entities that employ between 50 and 150 employees must adopt written

45 GN 563, at 26316.

46 See Chapter VI, section 24 of the draft regulations.

47 Sec 26 of the draft regulations.

measures to promote equality and must report in writing thereon upon the written request of a national state department. It must also, on request of a member of the public, cause its plan to be made available for inspection at its offices. Entities with less than 50 employees must adopt written measures to promote equality and must report in writing thereon upon the written request of a national state department.

The most obvious question relating to these draft regulations is whether the SAHRC and the various state departments will have the capacity to rigorously assess and monitor compliance with the equality plans and progress reports.[48]

The draft regulations pertaining to the promotion of equality cannot be successfully implemented without the heavy involvement of the SAHRC. The SAHRC will have to do the heavy lifting with the management of the equality plans envisioned by the Equality Act in its current form. The draft regulations task the SAHRC with a number of duties in respect of the equality plans such as assessing whether the measures to be implemented will achieve the stated goals and objectives and assessing whether the measures adopted to monitor the implementation of the equality plans are appropriate amongst others.[49] This is bound to be a mammoth task for the SAHRC, as it will have to draft guidelines and codes to guide the entities that have to submit equality plans on how to actually compile these plans. Then it will have to assess and monitor the compliance of these entities with the Equality Act and its regulations, amongst other tasks.

In this section, we proceed from the assumption that the SAHRC will not in the foreseeable future be empowered to be able to deal with millions of submitted equality plans. We therefore argue for an alternative approach to promote equality in terms of the Equality Act. We argue for amendments to the Equality Act and the existing draft regulations in relation to the promotion of equality. The assumption we make here is that the designated enforcement body in terms of the draft regulations – the SAHRC – is simply not in a position to monitor compliance with the Act. The approach set out in this section asks much from civil society instead.

To reiterate, the Equality Act is a national law that applies to the entire South Africa, across all sectors and public and private spheres of life. The Act

48 Compare Jagwanth (2003) 36 *Connecticut Law Review* 725 744. More recently, the Auditor-General has lamented the high rate of non-compliance by national and provincial government with key legislation. *See* audit outcomes of national and provincial government departments available on https://www.gov.za/sites/default/files/speech_docs/Audit%20 Outcomes%202015-16%20PFMA%20Presentation.pdf (accessed 5 September 2025).

49 See sec 25 of the draft regulations.

is drafted in general language, to be applied context specifically for each individual case that may appear before the equality courts. The draft regulations on the promotion of equality are likewise drafted in general language, to be adapted by the particular organisations asked to develop equality plans. The amendments we propose here are also proposed in general terms, not only for the education sector. The general gist of this section is, however, directed at schools as a particularly apt sector of society for addressing the transformation of hearts and minds.

The following sections in the South African Equality Act, as it currently stands, require the promulgation of regulations relating to the promotion of equality:

> Section 25(3)(c): "... [T]he constitutional institutions ... are also competent to request from the Department [of Justice], in the prescribed manner, regular reports regarding the number of cases and the nature and outcome thereof".
>
> Section 25(4)(b): "All Ministers must within their available resources prepare and implement equality plans, in the prescribed manner, which must include a time frame for implementation and which must be formulated in consultation with the Minister of Finance".
>
> Section 25(5)(a): "These equality plans must be submitted to the SAHRC to be dealt with in the prescribed manner".
>
> Section 26: "Any person directly or indirectly contracting with the State or exercising public power must promote equality by making regular reports to the relevant monitoring authorities or institutions as may be provided in regulations".
>
> Section 27(2): "The Minister of Justice must develop regulations to require companies, closed corporations, partnerships, clubs, sports organisations, corporate entities and associations, in a manner proportionate to their size, resources and influence, to prepare equality plans or abide by prescribed codes of practice or report to a body or institution to promote equality".

The proposed amendments to the Equality Act and draft regulations set out in this section proceed from the assumption that the SAHRC and other possible monitoring agencies are not sufficiently staffed or resourced to undertake a comprehensive monitoring of submitted equality plans from every company, closed corporation, partnership, club, sport organisation, corporate entity and association, nor from every person directly or indirectly contracting with the state or exercising public power.

The changes we suggest to the South African Equality Act and draft regulations accompanying the Act would rather require these bodies to develop and then make their equality plans publicly available and accessible to the public. This may, for example, be done by publishing the plans online and having them available at the premises of the body to supply the plan when requested. Where a particular body fails to develop, or fails to make publicly available, or publishes an inadequate equality plan, it is proposed that the draft regulations should include a provision empowering the equality courts, on application by an appropriate interested entity, to order the preparation and publication of such an equality plan. It is well-established that the equality courts are not overburdened, and creating this additional role for the equality courts will unlikely lead to clogged court rolls. Empowering equality courts to oversee the development and implementation of equality plans would allow these courts to play a more significant role in combating systemic discrimination as well – which is one of the explicit aims of the Equality Act.

We also propose that Section 14 of the Equality Act in its current form should be amended to allow equality courts to take cognisance of the existence or non-existence of a respondent's equality plan, and whether the published equality plan is appropriate, in the determination of the fairness or unfairness of the alleged discrimination. Such an amendment would supplement the provision that already appears in Section 14 that equality courts must consider "(i) whether and to what extent the respondent has taken such steps as being reasonable in the circumstances to – (i) address the disadvantage which arises from or is related to one or more of the prohibited grounds; or (ii) accommodate diversity".

It would not be a stretch for equality courts to rule on the content of equality plans. They are already called upon to make value judgements in deciding on "fair" or "unfair" discrimination. In the context of disabled learners, in ruling on "reasonable accommodation", the equality courts are already to some extent devising equality plans. In the case of *Oortman* v *St Thomas Aquinas Private School & Bernard Langton*,[50] the Mpumalanga equality court ruled that the respondent school had to readmit the learner and had to reasonably accommodate the learner. The court made specific orders to allow for access for the learner in her wheelchair to the classroom, washbasin and toilet.[51]

An audit of all laws calling on entities to draft equality/equity plans should be considered and so should the coordination and harmonisation of similar duties created in related legislation, for example the Employment Equity Act[52] which requires employers to submit employment equity plans that

50 Equality Court Case 1/2010 (December 2010).

51 Grobbelaar-Du Plessis I & Grobler (2013) 1 *African Disability Rights Yearbook* 307 320.

52 Act 55 of 1998.

must indicate how affirmative action measures will be implemented[53] and the Women Empowerment and Gender Equality Bill[54] which requires designated bodies to submit annual compliance plans on gender education; women's health care and reproductive health; public education on prohibited practices, including gender violence and equal representation and participation in decision-making.[55] The reporting obligations in these laws must be coordinated and harmonised so that all the relevant laws require one plan with the same content and same reporting cycle. Alternatively, those sections of other Acts calling for the preparation of equality/equity plans should be deleted, so as to create one overarching reporting duty.

We propose that all public and private bodies must prepare equality plans, irrespective of their size or influence. The preparation of an equality plan calls for consultation with affected communities and allows for reflection on how best to achieve substantive equality in a given context. Depending on the size and complexity of a particular public or private body, the preparation and content of an equality plan will vary significantly. A hairdresser's equality plan may amount to little more than a clearly visible sign posted at the entrance professing that all hair types are accommodated. On the other hand, as an example, a school's equality plan will have to address many interlocking and complex matters such as admission requirements, boarding placement policies, calculation of school fees, school culture, student governance structures, etc. To require small private entities to draft equality plans will therefore usually not be an onerous burden. To avoid the reporting obligations of larger bodies from becoming unduly onerous, one reporting obligation for all equality-related legislation should be created, as set out above. This would require an audit of all laws calling for equality/equity plans, and ensuring that these laws are harmonised.

An alternative approach would be to draft and prescribe codes of practice for particular sectors, for example education, service industry, sporting bodies, etc. to replace equality/equity plans. All entities operating in that particular sector would then be obliged to adhere to the relevant code of practice. These codes would have to be generic in nature, allowing each particular entity to interpret the applicable code in the context of its own operational and other requirements and circumstances. An opportunity to consult with the affected communities and stakeholders, and calling for the assistance of non-governmental

53 Sec 20 of the Employment Equity Act.

54 B50-2013.

55 Sec 4 of the Employment Equity Act.

organisations (NGOs) and civil society in drafting a tailor-made equality plan for that specific entity, would then be absent.

A number of proposed amendments to other sections in the Equality Act flow from this suggested approach (i.e. the preparation and publication of equality plans by all private and public entities, and empowering the equality courts to adjudicate on the content and implementation of equality plans).

In a similar fashion, we propose to require state departments to also prepare, publish and implement equality plans, but that these plans not be submitted to the SAHRC. (The SAHRC would still have its normal monitoring and other duties as prescribed in its founding legislation.)

Should the government accept this proposed model and amend the Equality Act and regulations accordingly, and bring into effect the promotional part of the Equality Act, schools and faculties of education at universities, governing bodies, educators, and learners will be significantly impacted.

The departments of basic and higher education, all universities, including faculties of education and all schools would have to develop equality plans; inter alia on how they would, over time, eliminate systemic discrimination, individual instances of unfair discrimination, hate speech and harassment related to the prohibited grounds in its area(s) of operation; illustrate how it will advance substantive equality in its area(s) of operation and illustrate how it will foster good relations in its area(s) of operation between persons who share a prohibited grounds and persons who do not. A consultative process would have to be followed to develop these plans. These plans must be developed in a bona fide, inclusive manner, allowing for input from all interested parties. These plans would then have to address matters such as *curricula* and assessment (the examples used and the questions asked); placement policies, codes of conduct, etc. – all in service of transforming schools into inclusive spaces and producing learners and young adults attuned to the imperatives of living up to and celebrating diversity, substantive equality and dignity.[56]

MEC for Education: Kwazulu-Natal v *Pillay*[57] involved a school who refused permission to a learner to wear a nose stud to school. The evidence showed that in terms of the learner's culture, wearing this nose stud was seen as celebrating the coming womanhood of the learner. The Constitutional Court held that the school's code of conduct unfairly discriminated against the learner for not allowing for exemptions to the code for inter alia bona fide cultural reasons.

56 See Kok *et al* (2020) 3 *Erasmus Law Review* 49 where an argument is made on how the disciplines of law and education can be used in conjunction to effect hearts and minds transformation, in the context of schools (and universities).

57 2007 2 SA 106 (CC).

The case did not directly deal with learners' hearts and minds, but some of the paragraphs in the judgment may be read as endorsing the approach set out in this book – an approach that would enforce difficult conversations in classrooms, where learners' diverse backgrounds and cultures and viewpoints are celebrated in such a way that the core values of the Constitution are strengthened;[58] in service of changing learners' hearts and minds.

International law also speaks directly to a duty on (South African) schools to promote equality in a much more thorough-going manner than is currently the case in classrooms. In terms of section 39(1)(b) of the Constitution, when interpreting the Bill of Rights, all South African courts must consider international law. The rights to substantive equality and education are explicitly guaranteed in the South African Bill of Rights; therefore, relevant international law principles are directly on point in how these rights (substantive equality read with the right to education) should be concretised.

The Abidjan Principles on the human rights obligations of states to provide public education and to regulate private involvement in education concretise in some detail what international human rights law on education implies for South African education law.[59] These principles were adopted in February 2019 in Côte d'Ivoire after a process of consultation and drafting that

58 For example, see paras 104: "Teaching the constitutional values of equality and diversity forms an important part of education. This approach not only teaches and promotes the rights and values enshrined in the Constitution, it also treats the learners as sensitive and autonomous people who can understand the impact the ban has on [the learner who was refused permission to wear a nose stud]"; 172: "A school is an ideal place to educate other learners about the difference between fashion and cultural practices and should an exemption for nose-studs be granted, a school would be obliged to furnish such education to its learners"; 173: "Schools are excellent institutions for creating the dialogue about culture that will best foster cultural rights in the overall framework of our Constitution. Schools that have diverse learner populations need to create spaces within the curriculum for diversity to be discussed and understood, but also they need to build processes to deal with disputes regarding cultural and religious rights that arise"; 185: "It is inevitable given the extraordinary transformation that the school in this case has undergone that conflict about the school and its rules should arise from time to time. It needs to be emphasised however, that the strength of our schools will be enhanced only if parents, learners and teachers accept that we all own our public schools and that we should all take responsibility for their continued growth and success. Where possible processes should be available in schools for the resolution of disputes, and all engaged in such conflict should do so with civility and courtesy. By and large school rules should be observed until an exemption has been granted. In this way, schools will model for learners the way in which disputes in our broader society should be resolved, and they will play an important role in realising the vision of the Preamble of our Constitution: a country that is united in its diversity in which all citizens are recognised as being worthy of equal respect".

59 www.abidjanprinciples.org/en/principles/overview (accessed 5 September 2025).

lasted three years.[60] The consultations involved legal practitioners, specialists in education and relevant community members from diverse localities.[61] One of the aims of the drafters of these principles was to explain what international human rights law implies for states in providing education.[62] Over the years, many bodies of the United Nations and other human rights institutions had been publishing a variety of documents on the topic, and there was a need to bring all of these together in a single document to confirm the ruling legal principles.[63]

Many of the Abidjan Principles speak directly to equality and discrimination and imply a duty on schools to ensure their learners inculcate appropriate values relating to inclusion and diversity. The first principle provides that "States must respect, protect, and fulfil the right to education of everyone within their jurisdiction in accordance with the rights to equality and non-discrimination". This principle is then spelt out in much detail in the explanatory document accompanying the principles. Speaking directly to the transformation of hearts and minds, the explanatory notes refer to four dimensions (our emphasis):

- a fair redistributive dimension to address socio-economic disadvantages;
- a recognition dimension to *combat stigma, stereotyping, prejudice*, and violence, and to *recognise the dignity of human beings* and the intersectionality of different grounds of discrimination;
- a participative dimension to *reaffirm the social nature of people* as members of social groups and the full recognition of humanity through inclusion in society; and
- a transformative dimension to *accommodate difference as a matter of human dignity* and institute systemic change.

The principles espoused in South African and international law require a pro-inclusion and pro-diversity approach. In our view, such a pro-inclusion and pro-diversity approach may be facilitated by the amendments proposed to the Equality Act in this section.

The current section 27 of the Equality Act should be broadened. The changes indicated below (strike-outs and insertions) reflect our proposed amendments to the current section:

> The Minister must develop regulations in relation to this Act ~~and other Ministers may develop regulations in relation to other Acts~~ which require *any*

60 www.abidjanprinciples.org/ (accessed 5 September 2025).

61 www.abidjanprinciples.org/en/background/overview (accessed 5 September 2025).

62 www.abidjanprinciples.org/ (accessed 5 September 2025).

63 www.abidjanprinciples.org/en/background/overview (accessed 5 September 2025).

> *person directly or indirectly contracting with the State or exercising public power, non-governmental organisations, community-based organisations, traditional institutions*, companies, closed corporations, partnerships, clubs, sports organisations, corporate entities and associations~~, where appropriate~~, in a manner proportional to their size, resources and influence, to prepare *and publish* equality plans ~~or abide by prescribed codes of practice or report to a body or institution on measures~~ to *advance* ~~promote~~ equality.

As explained above, section 14 of the Act contains a list of factors that an equality court must consider to decide if the impugned discrimination was fair or unfair. The additions we propose will allow an equality court to consider the relevance and content of a respondent's equality plan (or inadequate plan or absence of an equality plan) in determining if the alleged discrimination was fair or unfair:

> Section 14(3):
>
> (j) Whether the respondent has developed an equality plan or not;
>
> (k) If the respondent has developed an equality plan –
>
> whether this plan sets out how systemic unfair discrimination, individual instances of unfair discrimination, hate speech and harassment will be eliminated over time; whether this plan sets out how good relations will be fostered between persons who share a prohibited ground and persons who do not share it; whether the plan's goals and objectives are directed towards the advancement of equality; whether the measures to be implemented will achieve the stated goals and objectives; whether the measures adopted to monitor the implementation of the equality plan are appropriate; whether the criteria to evaluate the implementation of the equality plan are appropriate; whether the equality plan will achieve reasonable progress towards the eradication of systemic discrimination and the advancement of equality; whether time frames have been set and/or met and if not whether cogent reasons have been provided for this omission and whether measures have been put in place to expedite the implementation of the equality plan.

The sections in the Act dealing with the nature of the enquiry that an equality court may undertake and the remedies an equality court may order should also be expanded, to allow an equality court to inquire into the existence of equality plans and, where required, order the preparation, publication or implementation of equality plans:

Section 20(2)

Proceedings under section 21(1)(e), (f) and (g) may be instituted by any of the persons or associations listed in section 20(1) as well as the South African Human Rights Commission, the Commission for Gender Equality or the Director-General of the relevant State department.

Section 21

(1) The equality court before which proceedings are instituted in terms of or under this Act must hold an inquiry in the prescribed manner and determine whether one or more of the following has taken place, as alleged:

a) unfair discrimination
b) hate speech
c) harassment
d) the publication of material that illustrates the intention to unfairly discriminate
e) the omission to prepare an equality plan as required in terms of this Act and any regulations promulgated in terms of this Act
f) the omission to publish an equality plan as required in terms of this Act and any regulations promulgated in terms of this Act
g) the omission to adequately implement an equality plan

Section 21(2)[64]

...

(b) a declaratory order, including a declaratory order whether sufficient progress has been made with theimplementation of the respondent's equality plan and/or the measures to expedite theimplementation of the respondent's equality plan

...

(q) an order to prepare an equality plan in terms regarded appropriate by the court and as required in terms of this Act and any regulations promulgated in terms of this Act

(r) an order to publish an equality plan in terms regarded appropriate by the court and as required in terms of this Act and any regulations promulgated in terms of this Act

64 Sec 21(2) lists the remedies an equality court may order.

(s) an order to take appropriate measures to expedite the implementation of the respondent's equality plan

The equality plans that state departments and private bodies should develop and publish should be prescribed to contain, *inter alia*:

a) illustrate how it will, over time, eliminate systemic unfair discrimination, and individual instances of unfair discrimination, hate speech and harassment related to the prohibited grounds in its area(s) of operation;
b) illustrate how it will advance substantive equality in its area(s) of operation;
c) illustrate how it will foster good relations in its area(s) of operation between persons who share a prohibited ground and persons who do not;
d) contain specific and measurable objective(s), timeframes for the implementation of each objective, the mechanisms to monitor the implementation of each objective and the criteria to evaluate the implementation of the equality plan.
e) be prepared after consultation with affected communities and affected business sectors through any appropriate means;
f) contain specific and measurable objective(s), timeframes for the implementation of each objective, the mechanisms to monitor the implementation of each objective and the criteria to evaluate the implementation of the equality plan;
g) within 30 days after the signing thereof, the document shall be circulated under the signature of the chief executive officer of the entity to all its employees and made available for inspection at each of its offices and on its website, if any.

The regulations to the Equality Act should also prescribe a clear process to be followed in developing equality plans to ensure that inclusive, participatory processes are followed to allow for substantive input from internal and external stakeholders, civil society and NGOs.

The Department of Basic Education should also embed principles of substantive equality and equality law in the curriculum from the first to last school year of all public and private schools.[65]

The approach suggested in this section demands much from the state, private bodies and individuals. It also presupposes a capacitated state with strong monitoring powers, and wise bureaucrats and judges who are committed to a pro-inclusion and pro-diversity project, in service of facilitating the creation of a kind and caring society.

65 See www.reaseheath.ac.uk/wp-content/uploads/2012/05/Equality-Curriculum-Handbook.pdf for possible approaches to this proposal (accessed 5 September 2025).

CHAPTER 8

Conclusion

We explored ways in which law, and particularly equality jurisprudence, grapples with acts that are often dismissed as trivial, yet which cumulatively inflict deep harm. By undertaking a comparative survey of the *de minimis* principle in Germany, Canada, New Zealand, the Netherlands, and Namibia, and by focusing strongly on the South African experience, we have shown that what the law treats as "too small" to matter is never neutral. Decisions about triviality are themselves value-laden and reflect broader social hierarchies.

South Africa's constitutional order is rooted in a history of both large-scale systemic oppression and the daily humiliations of apartheid. Post-1994, Parliament and the courts were tasked not only with dismantling overt structures of racism, sexism, and homophobia, but also with addressing the more subtle indignities and humiliations that corrode dignity and equality over time. The challenge has been to determine whether, and how, the law should intervene in such cases without trivialising the judiciary or overburdening the system.

Throughout the book, we have argued that dismissing micro-aggressions under the *de minimis non curat lex* principle fails to recognise their cumulative and systemic effect. Far from being inconsequential, these everyday slights reinforce exclusion and sustain inequality. Courts and legislatures should thus be cautious about too readily invoking triviality. Instead, they should develop nuanced approaches that balance freedom of expression with the right to equality and dignity, and that acknowledge how power dynamics shape whether an insult or slight can be brushed off or not.

We have also proposed several reforms and strategies: the equality courts in South Africa should be resourced and empowered to address everyday discrimination more effectively; education and awareness campaigns should shift cultural understandings of micro-aggressions; and doctrinal development should recognise the symbolic and transformative potential of adjudicating even "small" cases of humiliation. Comparative insights demonstrate that while no jurisdiction has found a perfect balance, the South African framework, if strengthened, offers a promising model for combining legal redress with broader societal change.

In closing, the book underscores that law cannot solve every instance of discrimination or indignity, but neither should it abdicate responsibility for the "daily pinpricks" that shape people's lived experience. If the constitutional

 | HTTPS://DOI.ORG/10.1163/9789004757523-009

promise of dignity and equality is to be meaningful, legal systems must remain attentive not only to the spectacular harms of violence and exclusion, but also to the quieter, more insidious practices of marginalisation. In this lies the transformative potential of equality law: to affirm that every person matters, even in the smallest of encounters.

Bibliography

Canada

Statutes

Canadian Charter of Rights and Freedoms.
Human Rights Act R.S.C., 1985, c. H-6.

Case Law

Basi v. Canadian National Railway Co. (No. 1) (1988), 9 CHRR D/5029 (CHRT).
Bilac v Abbey and Others, 2023 CHRT 43 (CanLII).
Dion v R 2020 (CanLII) 3049 (QCCS).
Fitzgerald v Toronto Police Services Board 2019 HRTO 22.
Nielsen v Nee Tahi Buhn Indian Band, 2019 CHRT 50 (CanLII).
R v Harding, 2001 (CanLII) 28036 ON SC.
R v Keegstra, 1990 (CanLII) 24 (SCC); (1990) 3 RCS.
Saskatchewan Human Rights Commission v Whatcott 2013 SCC 11, [2013] 1 SCR 467.

Publications

Building a Foundation for Change: Canada's Anti-Racism Strategy 2019–2022, Catalogue no. CH37-4/29-2019E, ISBN 978-0-660-31004-6.
Discussion paper on systemic racism in 2023, Cat. No.: HR4-100/2023E-PDF, ISSN: 978-0-660-49407-4.

England

Case Law

Gill and Another v El Vino Co Ltd 1983 1 All ER 398.
R v Perry (1845) 169 ER 154.

 | HTTPS://DOI.ORG/10.1163/9789004757523-010

Germany

Statutes

Criminal Code in the version published on 13 November 1998 (Federal Law Gazette I, p. 3322), as last amended by Article 2 of the Act of 22 November 2021 (Federal Law Gazette I, p. 4906).

General Act on Equal Treatment of 14 August 2006 (Federal Law Gazette I, p. 1897), as last amended by Article 4 of the Act of 19 December 2022 (Federal Law Gazette I, p. 2510).

Case Law

BGH [1994] NJW 1421.

LAG Schleswig-Holstein, judgment of 23.12.2009, 6 Sa 158/09.

Namibia

Statutes

Racial Discrimination Prohibition Act 26 of 1991.

Racial Discrimination Prohibition Amendment Act 26 of 1998.

Case Law

S v Smith and Others 1996 NR 367 (HC).

Publications

National Human Rights Action Plan: Republic of Namibia: 2015–2019 https://ombudsman.org.na/wp-content/uploads/2022/09/NHRAP.pdf (accessed on 29 May 2025).

Netherlands

Statutes

General Equal Treatment Act (AWGB).

Case Law

ECLI:NL:GHDHA:2023:2911.
ECLI:NL:HR:2021:1036 Supreme Court, 06-07-2021, 20/03005.
ECLI:NL:RBDHA:2022:2537.

Publications

College voor de Rechten van de Mens, *Jaarverslag 2023*, April 2024 https://publicaties.mensenrechten.nl/publicatie/138c98d0-137d-4b3d-a718-b724bcedb16b (accessed 29 May 2025).

Dutch Ministry of the Interior and Kingdom Relations, *National Action Plan on Human Rights*, February 2014 https://www.humanrights.dk/sites/humanrights.dk/files/media/document/Netherlands%20NHRAP%202014%20English.pdf (accessed on 29 May 2025).

New Zealand

Statutes

Human Rights Act 82 of 1993.

Case Law

Quilter v Attorney-General [1997] NZCA 207; [1998] 1 NZLR 523.
Singh v McKee [2024] NZHRRT 3.
Wall v Fairfax New Zealand Ltd [2018] NZHC 104.

Publications

New Zealand Council for Educational Research, *A rapid review of racism in schools: Working paper*, 2020 https://wellbeingatschool.org.nz/sites/default/files/documents/Racism-in-schools-Rapid-review-working-paper_0.pdf (accessed 29 May 2025).

New Zealand Human Rights Commission, *Community Engagement Report for developing a National Action Plan Against Racism*, November 2022 https://tikatangata.org.nz/cms/assets/Documents/Reports-and-Inquiry/Race-and-Ethnicity/Large-Print_Ki-te-whaiao-ke-te-ao-Marama_Summary-Report_PDF.pdf (accessed 31 May 2025).

South Africa

Statutes

The Constitution of the Republic of South Africa, 1996.
The Employment Equity Act 55 of 1998.
The Promotion of Equality and Prevention of Unfair Discrimination Act 4 of 2000.

Case Law

Afriforum v Economic Freedom Fighters and others 2024 6 SA 1 (SCA).
Afri-Forum and Another v Malema and Others (20968/2010) [2011] ZAEQC 2.
Benoni Town Council v Meyer & Others 1961 3 SA 316 (W).
Campbell Scientific Africa (Pty) Ltd v Simmers [2016] 1 BLLR 1 (LAC).
Communication Specialists CC v Poulter (CA 540/2002) 2003 ZAECHC 1.
De Lange v Costa [1989] 2 All SA 267 (A).
Du Preez v The Minister of Justice and Constitutional Development 2006 5 SA 5922 (EqC).
Gaum and Others v Van Rensburg NO and Others [2019] 2 All SA 722 (GP).
Harksen v Lane 1998 1 SA 300 (CC).
Herselman v Geleba (231/2009) [2011] ZAECGHC 108.
Le Roux v Dey 2011 3 SA 274 (CC).
Lourens v Speaker of the National Assembly of Parliament and Others [2016] 2 All SA 340 (SCA).
Maharaj v National Horseracing Authority of Southern Africa 2008 4 SA 59 (N).
Manong and Associates (Pty) Ltd v Eastern Cape Department of Roads and Transport & Others 2009 6 SA 589 (SCA).
Masiu v Dos Ramos (A217/11) 2012 ZAFSHC 79.
Masuku and Another v South African Human Rights Commission obo South African Jewish Board of Deputies 2019 2 SA 194 (SCA).
MEC for Education: Kwazulu-Natal v *Pillay* 2007 2 SA 106 (CC).
Minister of Environmental Affairs and Tourism v George and Others 2007 3 SA 62 (SCA).
Minister of Finance v Van Heerden 2004 6 SA 121 (CC).
Osman v Minister of Safety and Security and Others (EC09/2008) [2010] ZAEQC 1.
Pharmavalu Sunnyside BK and Others v Pretorius (A200/2009) [2010] ZAGPPHC 114.
Pillay v MEC for Education, KwaZulu-Natal, and Others 2006 6 SA 363 (EqC).
Pillay v MEC for Education, KwaZulu-Natal, and Others 2006 10 BCLR 1237 (N).
Pretorius and Others v Minister of Justice and Correctional Services and Others 2018 2 SACR 501 (GP).
R v Dane 1957 2 SA 472 (N).
R v Maguire 1964 4 SA 191 (RA).
R v Walton 1958 3 SA 693 (SR).

S v Jordan 2002 6 SA 642 (CC).
S v Kgogong 1980 3 SA 600 (A).
S v Mostert 2006 1 SACR 560 (N).
S v Neotel (Pty) Ltd 2019 1 SA 622 (GJ).
S v Seweya 2004 1 SACR 387 (T).
S v Steenberg 1999 1 SACR 594 (N).
S v Van der Merwe 2011 2 SACR 509 (FB).
S v Visagie 2009 2 SACR 70 (W).
SAHRC obo South African Jewish Board of Deputies v Masuku and Another 2018 3 SA 291 (GJ).
Singh v Minister of Justice and Constitutional Development and Others 2013 3 SA 66 (EqC).
Sonke Gender Justice Network v Malema 2010 7 BCLR 729 (EqC).
South African Human Rights Commission v Khumalo 2019 1 SA 289 (GJ).
South African Human Rights Commission v Qwelane (44/EQJHB) [2011] ZAEQC.
Strydom v Chiloane 2008 2 SA 247 (T).
Strydom v Nederduitse Gereformeerde Gemeente Moreleta Park [2008] ZAGPHC 269; (2009) 30 ILJ 868 (EqC).
Thembani v Swanepoel 2017 3 SA 70 (ECM).

United States of America

Case Law

Ballin v Los Angeles County Fair 43 Cal.App.2d Supp. 884 (1941).
Boyd v United States 116 U.S. 616 (1886).
City of Clearwater v. Studebaker's Dance Club 516 So.2d 1106 (Fla. Dist. Ct. App. 1987).
Elk Grove Unified School District v Newdow 542 U.S. 1 (2004).
Harris v Time 191 Cal.App.3d 449 (1987).
Hessel v O'Hearn 977 F.2d 299 (7th Cir. 1992).
Koire v Metro Car Wash 707 P.2d 195 (1985).
Ladd v Iowa West Racing Association 443 N.W.2d 600 (Iowa 1989).
Lewis v Woods 848 F.2d 649 (5th Cir. 1988).
Pennsylvania Liquor Control Board v. Dobrinoff 471 A.2d 941 (1984).
Peppin v Woodside Delicatessen 506 A.2d 263 (Md. Ct. Spec. App. 1986).
Pulman Co v Dudley 77 S.W.2d 592, 593 (Tex. Civ. App. 1934).
Raymon v Alvord Independent School District et al 639 F.2d 257 (1981).
Sentell v New Orleans & Carrollton Railroad Company 166 U.S. 698 (1897).
Wisconsin Department of Revenue v William Wrigley Jr Co 505 U.S. 1992 214.

Scholarly Books, Research Papers and Journal Articles

Allport G (1979) *The Nature of Prejudice* Basic Books.

Bell M & Cormack J (2005) *Developing Anti-Discrimination Law in Europe – The 25 EU Member States Compared* available at https://www.migpolgroup.com/_old/portfolio/developing-anti-discrimination-law-in-europe-the-25-eu-member-states-compared/ (accessed on 31 May 2025).

Bernstein A "Civil Rights = Broken Windows: *De Minimis Curet Lex*" (2010) 62 *Florida Law Review* 895.

Böcker A "Can Non-Discrimination Law Change Hearts and Minds" (2020) 3 *Erasmus Law Review* 21.

Bohler N "Equality Courts: Introducing the Possibility of Listening to Different Voices in South Africa?" (2000) 63 *Journal of Contemporary Roman-Dutch Law* 288.

Bohler-Muller N "What the Equality Courts can Learn from Gilligan's Ethic of Care: A Novel Approach" (2000) 16 *South African Journal on Human Rights* 623.

Botes A "Sexual harassment as a ground for dismissal: A critical evaluation of the labour and labour appeal courts' decisions in Simmers v Campbell Scientific Africa" (2017) *Tydskrif vir die Suid-Afrikaanse Reg* 761.

Brand D "Die Wet op die Bevordering van Gelykheid en die Voorkoming van Onbillike Diskriminasie" (2000) Autumn *Word and Action* 13.

Brown J "How much is too much? The application of the de minimis doctrine to the fourth amendment" (2013) 82 *Mississippi Law Journal* 1097.

De Vos P "Equality for all? A critical analysis of the equality jurisprudence of the Constitutional Court" (2000) 63 *Journal of Contemporary Roman-Dutch Law* 67.

De Vos P "Sexual orientation and the right to equality in the South African Constitution: National Coalition for Gay and Lesbian Equality and another v Minister of Justice and Others" (2000) 117 *South African Law Journal* 17.

Dror Y "Law and Social Change" (1958) 33 *Tulane Law Review* 787.

Ford TE, Boxer CF, Armstrong J & Edel JR "More than 'Just a Joke': The prejudice releasing function of sexist humor" (2007) 34 *Personality & Social Psychology Bulletin* 159.

Fredman S "Providing equality: Substantive equality and the positive duty to provide" (2005) 21 *South African Journal on Human Rights* 163.

Grobbelaar-Du Plessis I & Grobler C "South Africa" (2013) 1 *African Disability Rights Yearbook* 307.

Guthrie WD (1898) *Lectures on the fourteenth article of amendment to the Constitution of the United States Lecture II: The principles of construction and interpretation* Little, Brown and Company Boston.

Gutto SBO (2001) *Equality and Non-Discrimination in South Africa: The Political Economy of Law and Law Making* New Africa Books Claremont.

Hocking BA "Where are We After 10 Years of Discrimination Law?" (1995) 15 *Proctor* 19.

Hoctor S "*De minimis not curat lex*" (2012) 80 *e-Mantshi* 9 available at http://www.justiceforum.co.za/JET-LTN.ASP#:~:text=e%2DMantshi%20%C2%A0%20Issue%2080%20September%202012%20%2D%20560kb (accessed 5 September 2025).

Holley L & Steiner S "Safe space: Student perspectives on classroom environment" (2005) 1 *Journal of Social Work Education* 49.

Inest A "A theory of de minimis and a proposal for its application in copyright" (2006) 21 *Berkeley Technology Law Journal* 945.

Jagwanth CF "Affirmative action in a transformative context: The South African experience" (2003) 36 *Connecticut Law Review* 738.

Karst KL "'A Discrimination So Trivial': A Note on Law and the Symbolism of Women's Dependency" (1974) 35 *Ohio State Law Journal* 546.

Klare KE "Legal Culture and Transformative Constitutionalism" (1998) 14 *South African Journal on Human Rights* 146.

Kok JA *A socio-legal analysis of the Promotion of Equality and Prevention of Unfair Discrimination Act 4 of 2000* 2008 LLD thesis University of Pretoria.

Kok JA, Xaso L, Steenekamp A & Oelofse M "The Promotion of Equality and Prevention of Unfair Discrimination Act 4 of 2000: Proposals for Legislative Reform to Promote Equality through Schools and the Education System" (2020) 3 *Erasmus Law Review* 49.

Kruger R "Small steps to equal dignity: The work of the South African Equality Courts" (2011) 7 *The Equal Rights Review* 27.

Labuschagne JMT "De Minimis Non Curat Lex" (1973) *Acta Juridica* 291.

Landreman LM (ed) (2013) *The art of effective facilitation: Reflections from social justice educators* Routledge New York.

Langa P "Transformative constitutionalism" (2006) 17 *Stellenbosch Law Review* 351.

Liebenberg S & O'Sullivan M "South Africa's new equality legislation: A tool for advancing women's socio-economic equality?" (2001) *Acta Juridica* 70.

Lukes R & Bangs J "A critical analysis of anti-discrimination law and microaggressions in academia" (2014) 24 *Research in Higher Education Journal* 3.

McKean FG "De minimis non curat lex" (1926–1927) 75 *University of Pennsylvania Law Review* 429.

Moseneke D "The Fourth Bram Fischer Memorial Lecture: Transformative Adjudication" (2002) 18 *South African Journal on Human Rights* 309.

Neethling J "Personality rights: A Comparative Overview" (2005) 38 *Comparative and International Law Journal of Southern Africa* 220.

Nemerofsky J "What is a trifle anyway?" (2001–2002) 37 *Gonzaga Law Review* 315.

Newman RK "School prayer and the ten commandments" (1998) 28 *Cumberland Law Review* 1.

Oxford Pro Bono Publico (2012) *Comparative hate speech law: Annexure* available at https://www.law.ox.ac.uk/sites/files/oxlaw/1a._comparative_hate_speech_annex.pdf (accessed 5 September 2025).

Pierce CM (1978) *Television and education* Sage: University of California.

Pieterse M "Cases and comments: Discrimination through the eye of the beholder" (2000) 16 *South African Journal on Human Rights* 121.

Pieterse M "What do we mean when we talk about transformative constitutionalism" (2005) 20 *Southern African Public Law* 155.

Rank JE "Is ladies' night really sex discrimination?: Public accommodation laws, de minimis exceptions, and stigmatic injury" (2005–2006) 36 *Seton Hall Law Review* 223.

Ross-Amato J "Transgender Employees and Restroom Designation" (2002–2003) 29 *William Mitchell Law Review* 569.

Samuels A "De Minimus Non Curat Lex" (1985) *Statute Law Review* 167.

Sasso GL "Class actions: De minimis curat lex?" (2004–2005) 31 *Litigation* 16.

Snyman CR "Voorwaardes vir strafregtelike aanspreekliheid buite onreg en skuld" (2002) *Journal of South African Law* 139.

Snyman CR "Watering the dagga pot-plant: A questionable reward" (1975) 92 *South African Law Journal* 372.

Sue DW, Capodilupo CM, Torino GC, Bucceri JM, Holder AMB, Nadal KL & Esquilin M "Racial microaggressions in everyday life: Implications for clinical practice" (2007) 62 *American Psychologist* 271.

Tutu DM *No future without forgiveness* (1999) New York: Doubleday.

Veech ML & Moon CR "De minimis non curat lex" (1947) 45 *Michigan Law Review* 537.

Verwoerd W and Verwoerd M "On the Injustice of (Un)just Joking" (1994) 23 *Agenda* 67.

White R "De Minimis Discrimination" (1998) 47 *Emory Law Journal* 1121.

Woolman S & Bishop M (eds) 2014 *Constitutional Law of South Africa* 2nd ed Juta Cape Town.

Internet, Newspaper Articles and Popular Media

Archer J (2024) "10 benefits of kindness" available at https://www.psychreg.org/10-benefits-kindness/ (accessed 5 September 2025).

BBC 2019 "France harassment law hands out 447 fines in first months" available at https://www.bbc.com/news/world-europe-48104247 (accessed 5 September 2025).

Canadian Centre for Diversity and Inclusion (2017) "Diversity & inclusion councils: Toolkit for diversity and inclusion practitioners" available at https://ccdi.ca/media/1072/20170831-ccdi-diversity-council-toolkit-final-v3.pdf (accessed on 29 May 2025).

Coldwell C "Some trifles do concern the law" *Financial Times* July 24 2009.

Donegan M (2019) "So Joe Biden's not a pussy grabber. Is that really good enough?" available at https://www.theguardian.com/commentisfree/2019/apr/02/joe-biden-inapprorpriate-touching-lucy-flores?CMP=Share_iOSApp_Other (accessed 5 September 2025).

Ellis-Petersen H (2019) "Have you heard about the Philippine mayor who banned gossip?" available at https://www.theguardian.com/world/2019/may/01/have-you-heard-about-the-philippine-mayor-who-banned-gossip?CMP=Share_iOSApp_Other (accessed 5 September 2025).

Ford RT (2011) "Should ladies' nights really be illegal?" available at http://www.slate.com/articles/news_and_politics/jurisprudence/features/2011/should_ladies_nights_really_be_illegal_an_excerpt_from_richard_t/week_1/should_ladies_nights_really_be_illegal_an_excerpt_from_richard_t_1.html#correction (accessed 5 September 2025).

Hanley-Dafoe R (2023) "Why kindness matters" available at https://www.psychologytoday.com/us/blog/everyday-resilience/202303/the-remarkable-power-of-kindness-and-why-it-matters (accessed 5 September 2025).

Hytner M (2019) "Israel Folau to be sacked by Rugby Australia over social media posts" available at https://www.theguardian.com/sport/2019/apr/11/israel-folau-to-be-sacked-by-rugby-australia-over-social-media-posts?CMP=Share_iOSApp_Other (accessed 5 September 2025).

Journalists for Justice (2023) "Dutch border controls illegally discriminate against black people, court rules" available at https://jfjustice.net/dutch-border-controls-illegally-discriminate-against-black-people-court-rules/ (accessed 29 May 2025).

McGann L (2019) "Lucy Flores isn't alone. Joe Biden has a long history of touching women inappropriately" available at https://www.vox.com/policy-and-politics/2019/3/29/18241598/joe-biden-lucy-flores-touching-women-media-history-explained (accessed 5 September 2025).

Ottawa Public Health (2025) "Have THAT *talk about racism*" available at https://www.ottawapublichealth.ca/en/public-health-services/have-that-talk-about-racism.aspx#Have-THAT-talk-about-racism-activity-guide (accessed 29 May 2025).

Robinson M (2019) "Upskirting is now a crime in England and Wales – offenders face up to 2 years in jail" available at https://edition.cnn.com/2019/04/12/uk/upskirting-uk-criminal-offense-intl-scli-gbr/ (accessed 5 September 2025).

Schiller C (2023) "Kindness can be positively powerful – here's why" available at https://healthtalk.unchealthcare.org/kindness-can-be-positively-powerful-heres-why/ (accessed 5 September 2025).

Skrzypinski C (2023) "Canada: HR Should Address Microaggressions in DE&I Training" available at https://www.shrm.org/topics-tools/news/canada-hr-address-microaggressions-dei-training (accessed 29 May 2025).

Sue DW (2010) "Microaggressions: More Than Just Race" available at https://www.psychologytoday.com/us/blog/microaggressions-in-everyday-life/201011/microaggressions-more-just-race (accessed 5 September 2025).

Toronto Metropolitan University Diversity Institute (2021) "The Micropedia of Microaggressions Launches to Shed Light on a Subtle but Commonly Experienced

Form of Discrimination" available at https://www.torontomu.ca/diversity/news-events/2021/12/the-micropedia-of-microaggressions-launches-to-shed-light-on-a-s/ (accessed on 29 May 2025).

Van Gelder L (2020) "Institutional racism is a Dutch problem too" available at https://universonline.nl/nieuws/2020/06/16/institutional-racism-dutch-problem/ (accessed 29 May 2025).

Index

 | HTTPS://DOI.ORG/10.1163/9789004757523-011

www.ingramcontent.com/pod-product-compliance
Lightning Source LLC
Chambersburg PA
CBHW071353230926
51846CB00002B/541
* 9 7 8 9 0 0 4 7 5 7 5 1 6 *